THE MESSAGE

THE MESSAGE

Gerry Griffin and Andy Lark

Matador
BUSINESS

Copyright © 2010 Gerry Griffin and Andy Lark

The moral right of the author has been asserted.

Apart from any fair dealing for the purposes of research or private study, or criticism or review, as permitted under the Copyright, Designs and Patents Act 1988, this publication may only be reproduced, stored or transmitted, in any form or by any means, with the prior permission in writing of the publishers, or in the case of reprographic reproduction in accordance with the terms of licences issued by the Copyright Licensing Agency. Enquiries concerning reproduction outside those terms should be sent to the publishers.

Matador Business
5 Weir Road
Kibworth Beauchamp
Leicester LE8 0LQ, UK
Tel: (+44) 116 279 2299
Email: books@troubador.co.uk
Web: www.troubador.co.uk/matador

ISBN 978-1848763-753

A Cataloguing-in-Publication (CIP) catalogue record for this book is available from the British Library.

Typeset in 11pt Palatino by Troubador Publishing Ltd, Leicester, UK
Printed in Great Britain by the MPG Books Group, Bodmin and King's Lynn

Matador
Matador Business is an imprint of Troubador Publishing Ltd

For Kristen – whose messages remain a source of inspiration.

Contents

Acknowledgements ix
Foreword xi
Introduction xiii

1	Message received?	1
2	Communicating in a connected age	19
3	Anatomy of a message	33
4	Time to deliver	53
5	On the campaign trail	69
6	Welcome to The Grid	87
7	The go-between	99
8	You've been framed	113
9	Conversations and transactions	129
10	Seeking inspiration?	145
11	A personal connection	161
12	What's the story?	179

Ten Key Ideas 201

Acknowledgements

Many thanks to Steve Coomber and Dr Ciaran Parker. To the thinking man's thinker Stuart Crainer and of course Bronagh, James and DJ.

With deep gratitude to Kristen, Sophia and Zach who have tolerated too many weekends of research. To all the team at Dell for their constant insights and conversations. And to the bloggers and streamers whose river of insights and information are a constant source of inspiration.

Foreword

Is happiness an empty inbox? A day without news? Being able to cut through the stream of babble that has come to dominate our social media sites?

Yes, we are in a world of information overload. In the Attention Economy discrimination between chatter, information and critical communication is at a premium. The ability to "cut through" with messages that are as compelling as they are memorable will separate the most powerful communicators from the rest.

The Message will help with this. We need to focus, channel and direct what we say; how we say it and the where we choose to say it.

We are in an exciting tower of babel – with many voices competing for share of attention. In this book we aim to give you the tools and the examples to help make a difference

Enjoy

Andy Lark, Gerry Griffin
December 2009

Introduction

Written messages have been around for a long time. Many thousands of years. Like the written messages on the Ebers Papyrus, dating back to about 1550 BC. Created by Ancient Egyptians, the papyrus details some interesting medical and household related tips, such as using the fat from cats to keep your best outfits safe from the unwanted attention of mice and rats.

Of course, messages date back earlier than the Ancient Egyptians, back to the beginning of language, no doubt. And, just as people have been communicating for thousands of years, so too have they been struggling to get the message they intended across.

In Ancient Sumer, for example, four thousand or so years before the birth of Christ, where the Sumerians were one of the most advanced civilisations of the time, there is evidence to suggest that women and men spoke different dialects of a similar language. So plenty of opportunity for confusion and misunderstanding in messages passed between the sexes.

Fast forward a few thousand years, and about 7,000 living languages, and communication appears to be more, rather than less, complicated. There are so many more ways to communicate. You can still write words on paper, or talk to people face-to-face. But why do that when you can email, text, phone – terrestrial, satellite,

THE MESSAGE

or standard mobile, broadcast on the television or radio, create a podcast, or videocast, and post it on the Internet. Why not instant message someone?

Individuals and organisations are both trying to create more personal, intimate and authentic messages, using blogs (weblogs), vlogs (video blogs), moblogs (mobile blogs), even flogs (fake blogs). But is anyone paying attention??

So many more ways to communicate; so many more ways to communicate badly. Blue skies thinking, thinking outside of the box, bandwidth, low-hanging fruit, people in business seem overly fond of the opaque, acronym-rich, jargon you tend to associate with business schools and MBAs.

With all the communication noise and all the jargon, it is no wonder organisations and individuals are struggling to get their messages across.

Take corporate mission statements. What is the point? To encapsulate the essence of the organisation's purpose, its reason for being; a concise rallying cry uniting employees in a common endeavour. They are also outward facing, signalling to the general populous, the consumer and other stakeholders, what the organisation is all about. That is the theory at least.

The reality is often a little different, as organisation's struggle to compile a message sufficiently concise to convey the intended meaning to an audience that demands brevity.

So an organisation that deals with the very latest advances in information and communications technology, IBM, decides on: "At

INTRODUCTION

IBM, we strive to lead in the invention, development and manufacture of the industry's most advanced information technologies, including computer systems, software, storage systems and microelectronics. We translate these advanced technologies into value for our customers through our professional solutions, services and consulting businesses worldwide."

And, while many organisations struggle to use messages effectively, the challenge grows more difficult by the year. After all, there is more information, by a considerable factor, but the same amount of time available to process it. So there has to be some sacrifice in terms of the way that we process information. What gets sacrificed is the ability to give every piece of information equal time and consideration. You may have weighted information before, filtered and prioritised. Now you have to, and far more than before, otherwise you become mired; bogged down in the information swamp.

To cope with the modern world we are developing shorter attention spans, for things that are not genuinely of interest, younger generations especially, and a bigger and broader attention span for anything that attracts interest and holds our attention.

Why should you care about using messages effectively? Because messages are at the heart of every organisation, of every career, of every relationship. Whether you are running a multinational corporation, or a small sales team; whether you are communicating with customers, constituents, colleagues or communities; whether you are speaking to suppliers or senior executives; mastery of the message is essential.

So in this book, we hope that we have provided a sense of what a message is, and some understanding of how to create, manage and deliver messages in the 21st century. And, in doing so, we hope that this understanding will enable you to create better messages, that communicate in a way that attracts interest and holds attention, to create messages that don't just disappear among all the noise, into the electronic ether.

Gerry Griffin & Andy Lark
London, 2009

ONE

Message Received

I Love You.

It was probably one the first messages you ever received. Wrapped in emotion; delivered with passion. It is the perfect message – but only if delivered in the right way, and at the right moment.

The impact hinges on delivery. Authenticity is critical. It is very difficult to fake. Without conviction or emotion these same three words are hollow and empty. And it's situational. Convey a message at the right moment and it elicits an immediate response; get the moment wrong and the message slips unnoticed beneath the tide of information we struggle against in our everyday lives.

Messages are an essential part of our everyday business lives. Business success hinges on the effective delivery of messages, both for organisations and the bottom line, and individuals, their performance and their career paths.

Organisations rely on messages to differentiate products and services. Without it value is depleted, products and services are neglected. Think of your favourite brands, companies, and people. In nearly every instance a simple and compelling message screams at you. Nike implores people to "Just Do It". BMW drives motorists to "The Ultimate Driving Machine".

For others the message is embedded in the brand values. The Virgin Group and its founder Sir Richard Branson embody values like Innovative, Competitively Challenging, and Fun. Equal doses of entertainment can be found at the highly successful US company Southwest Airlines, that over the years has distilled this same spirit to one word "Nuts!"

Just like the words "I Love You", messages by government and corporations need not be spelt out in black and white, emblazoned across billboards, or the first lines of every press release. Wherever they are written or spoken, however, the most effective messages are manifest in actions and behaviours of people. As the thousands of Virgin and Southwest Airlines employees do every day, they deliver the message through their actions.

In the same way that messages play an integral part in organisational success, whether it is communication internally within the organisation, or externally to the world, they also play an important part in the success of individual careers. Whether it is communicating with your bosses, with your team members, or with clients and customers, knowing how to use messages effectively is essential.

Rules of engagement

For decades marketers and activists have sought to craft the perfect message, and while many come close, perfection remains elusive.

MESSAGE RECEIVED

This is partly because the rules of engagement are constantly changing. For companies, the target for messages used to be a largely passive audience. That is no longer the case, though.

Today the rules for effective messaging extend beyond creating a message for the submissive many— they cover the sharing and receiving of messages as well. For we have entered a new "participatory era". Consumers are not content just to receive messages, but instead are keen to co-create, influence, react, and engage in conversations transactions, in short to participate. In this participation the consumer's weapons of choice are digital printing presses and streaming media channels. New rules of engagement call for new kinds of messaging.

This book is a messaging boot camp for the 21st century. It provides some insight into how messages are created, used and interacted with; and some practical what to do and what not to do pointers, for those people involved in creating and interacting with messages.

When you put the book down you should at least understand enough about messaging, and the essential role that messages play as part of everyday organisational and personal communication, to be able to improve your own message behaviour, and be able to deal with messaging on a more sophisticated level. What difference does that make? A lot. It could make the difference between corporate success and failure, the difference between career satisfaction and disappointment.

Note that this is a book about messaging in modern times, and the 21st century world that we live in brings its own unique set of challenges for messaging, a few of which are worth outlining upfront.

Message anxiety

It was Richard Saul Wurman, American architect and graphic designer, who coined the phrase Information Architect in 1975, and went on to explore Information Anxiety, our love-hate relationship with information, and to provide some practical strategies for controlling it both as consumers and producers.

If the barrage of information was bad in 1975, today it is many times worse as we are bombarded with messages. Email, websites, employers, TV, streaming video – the list seems endless. But it is not messaging overload per se that causes anxiety; it is being unable to find the message that you are looking for, or understand it when you do.

The first question that most consumers ask about a company, for example, is "what do you do"? It is one of the most common questions that an organisation will have to deal with and yet most companies do a fairly poor job of answering it. Trawl the websites of a few companies and you will soon discover how difficult they find it to express even the simplest of concepts.

Take the technology sector, for example, an industry that we have a lot of experience working with. When faced with trying to explain what their business does, many companies in the sector have a tendency to try to sound hip and sophisticated, but in doing so they deprive their potential customers of an opportunity to understand their business.

Curious consumers are likely to encounter phrases such as "technology solutions", "platforms", and "services orientated architectures". As a result, consumers are required to not only

MESSAGE RECEIVED

understand the company and product – all they really wanted to understand in the first place – but also a plethora of catch-phrases and buzzwords.

Individuals too, are fond of over complicating and obscuring messages. They talk in a jargon ridden private language, whether it is the kind of management speak cum business bullshit that gets drummed into you at business school doing an MBA, or the truncated text favoured by the instant messaging generation, devoid of vowels and inaccessible to a large segment of the population.

No wonder then that many of us suffer from message anxiety.

Message memo: Infomania

A recent survey, by secure messaging company Mirapoint, suggested that almost a quarter of all emails in corporate inboxes are personal. Take the personal email, add to it the junk mail, and the legitimate business related email, relevant or not, and it is surprising that anyone gets any work done at all.

The torrent of email revealed by the survey ties in with another study — 1,100 respondents — for tech giant Hewlett Packard, which reveals that some people are becoming addicted to email and text messages. The guilty workers exhibited a number of traits: they checked work messages at home or on holiday (62%); they always responded to an email "immediately" or as soon as possible (over 50%); they admitted that they would interrupt a meeting to respond to an email (21%).

If this sounds familiar you may be suffering from "infomania". This is

> not good. Dr Glenn Wilson, the University of London psychologist who carried out the study at the Institute of Psychiatry, found excessive use of technology reduces workers' intelligence.
>
> The infomaniacs showed a drop in IQ test performance, worse than that of recreational drug takers. Those distracted by incoming email and phone calls saw a ten point fall in their IQ. This is the twice that found in studies of the impact of smoking marijuana.
>
> Anyone who needs a good eight hours sleep should also beware; constantly breaking away from tasks to react to email or text messages causes similar effects on the mind as losing a night's sleep.
>
> And this is the audience you are trying to reach with your messages.

Capturing mindspace

Wurman proposed that every company should have a company story that "tells the world what your business is all about. It should be a tale of passion, triumph, motivation, and opportunity." He adds, however: "It shouldn't have anything to do with your company mission statement."

Capturing that tale of passion, triumph, motivation, and opportunity, is far from easy though. For example, marketers are inclined to focus on aspects of message creation such as creativity, proliferation, and media, where what they really need to be focusing on is what the consumer needs to hear in order to act. This is at the heart of effective messaging; great marketers start with the space in the mind of the audience that they want to occupy – how to capture

MESSAGE RECEIVED

the mind of the message recipient.

And this is where many organisations fail. Brands guru Al Ries, who coined the marketing term "positioning", describes the problem with respect to failed products thus: "These products didn't fail in the marketplace, they failed in the mind. They tried to stand for something that didn't fit prospects' perceptions about the brands."

Ries uses the example of the cola wars in the 1960s and 1970s to illustrate the point. Back in 1963, the Pepsi-Cola brand launched an advertising programme which is a great example of effective messaging.

Pepsi-Cola decided to use the core concept of "The Pepsi Generation," to underpin its product messages. This idea took advantage of a key psychological principle – that a younger generation will often search for ways of rebelling against the older generation. If the older generation were drinking Coca-Cola, then Pepsi-Cola's messaging claimed space in the minds of new customers that they should drink Pepsi to be a part of a new vibrant culture.

Great messages lay claim to mind share, and not just market share. Bad messages drive anxiety.

Talking about the "so what" generation

Overcoming message anxiety is by far from the only issue. Another challenge for communicators is dealing with different audiences, and in particular different generations.

Perhaps the most challenging generation to reach with messages is

THE MESSAGE

the "so what generation," more conventionally known as the Millennial generation (or Millennium generation), but also tagged as Generation Y, Nexters, the Nintendo generation, or the Echo Boomers.

The millennials are a very distinctive generation. They follow the Baby Boomers, roughly speaking those born between 1946 and the early 1960s, who are approaching retirement, and Generation X – early 1960s to 1980 – who are hitting their 40s.

The children of Millennial generation were born in 1980s and 1990s, the offspring of the Baby Boomers. To give an idea of the size of this generation, although estimates vary, depending on the start and end dates, the millennial generation numbers some 78 million or so Americans.

With most in their teens and twenties, they are conspicuous consumers; they like to buy stuff – a lot of stuff. Which is why, whatever part of an organisation you work in, (and whether you are millennial or not) the ability to communicate with this generation is important.

But creating messages for the millenials is not easy. While Baby Boomers are the first generation to grow up with the television, and Gen X has watched the television channels proliferate, the millennials have experienced an explosion in communications technology and media channels.

Satellite television, and then the Internet have transformed the way the millennials consume information and interact with the world. This generation is, unsurprisingly, the most technology literate generation yet. Statistics abound but as a snapshot, a 2006/2007

MESSAGE RECEIVED

survey of US millenials revealed that 97% owned a computer, 76% used instant messaging, 28% wrote a blog and 44% read blogs; 34% use Web sites as their primary source of news; and 15% of IM users are logged on 24 hours a day/7 days a week.[1]

As the number of ways to interact increases so the attention span decreases. From MTV music videos, to You Tube streaming videos, to Twittering, the amount of information that millenials are willing to consume from one source in one sitting appears to be steadily decreasing.

Long gone are the ritualistic gatherings of the family around the television for a particular programme, soon to be gone are the moments of shared cultural identity as the millenials leading, with the rest of us following, personalise the content we experience, watching and listening at times that suit our own busy schedules.

Is it a coincidence that the restlessness manifest in a generation at its most extreme is given a medical diagnosis Attention-Deficit/Hyperactivity Disorder (ADHD). In the UK the NHS Direct website states that the condition affects between 3 to 9% of school-aged children and young people. In the US the National Institute of Mental Health estimates that between 3 and 5%, or approximately 2 million children, have ADHD.

While the majority of millennials are fortunate enough not to suffer from a medically diagnosed attention deficit disorder, many still suffer from an attention deficit compared to previous generations. As a result, unless you grab their attention with meaningful information early on in any communication interaction the response

---

[1] Reynol Junco and Jeanna Mastrodicasa

you are likely to be met with is –"so what". Or as Catherine Tate's comic creation Lauren Cooper might say– "am I bovvered."

Of course it would be easier to ignore this generation entirely, but for the majority of organisations and individuals alike, that is not a viable course of action. These people are the consumers. They are the voters. They are the people that make up an important part of the organisations you work in. Indeed you may be one of them. So failure to engage with the millenials would be disastrous commercially and personally. Because these people are the future.

Message memo: Brevity is best

In the new world of messaging there is little room for the long and lengthy, the non-pithy, non-concise.

A couple of hundred years ago, when Dr Samuel Johnson, the author of *A Dictionary of the English Language* was writing his letters, and newspaper articles, people seemed to take great pride in writing long, elaborately constructed sentences, with many subordinate clauses, that went on and on... and on.

Today most people haven't got the time or inclination, to absorb messages in this way. In fact, when it comes to written text, many people barely have time to read at all.

A 2007 report *Reading at Risk* by the National Endowment for the Arts in the US, a nation which tends to drive trends in a large part of the western world at least, compiled results from over 40 studies by a range of organisations from universities to business groups, suggests that reading levels among young people have falling rapidly over the last twenty or so years.

Statistics that stood out from the report included the fact that: the average person between the ages of 15 and 24 in the US spends 2 to 2 1/2 hours a day watching television and just 7 minutes reading; almost half of Americans between the ages of 18 and 24 never read books for pleasure; only about a third of high school seniors read at a proficient level, a 13% decline since 1992.

Undoubtedly the myriad of information sources and communication choices competing for people's attention is making the difference here. And this is borne out by the another of the report's findings: that over 50% of middle and high school students use other media most or some of the time while reading – for example, 20% of the time spent reading is also spent watching television, playing video games, or using a computer.

Newspapers have picked up on this trend with articles becoming shorter in length and many papers offering print summaries or abstracts of pieces. Readers, when they do read, frequently skim across a large number of pieces rather than read a few pieces in depth.

As a result of these changes in reading behaviour the very notion of what is long and what is short has changed. So, for example, a one-pager letter which could be seen by some people as a relatively short letter. But if you were to put that into the body copy of an email, it would look like quite a long email. Then again, if someone was browsing that on their BlackBerry, it would look like a very long message, because it would go on for four or five pages.

So today, almost without exception, brevity is best.

A message defined

Let's take a closer look at the subject of this book. Just what is a message? At its most basic a message is one of the key tools for active communication. But to better understand what a message is, first let's look at how a message works and functions.

A message is one of the key ways of communicating with people; whether it is making a business presentation, a sales pitch, putting together some new product literature, crafting a corporate vision, or writing a best man's speech. In business, a message is a key component that drives business value.

One problem with communication, certainly within organisations, is that people regard communication as synonymous with the communications or public relations department. In other words it is commonly viewed as an activity that is the responsibility of a particular group of people within the organisation, and an activity that is divorced from the thousands of decisions that people take in work every day, and every hour.

This is nonsense. Yes, the communications and PR departments do play an important role in organisational communications, both externally and internally. But we all communicate, albeit for the most part not that effectively, as part of our business activities.

In a business context, communication, and within that the message, is used to make something happen. What that "something" is, varies considerably, but in work it is often about changing the behaviour or mindset of the audience to make it easier for business goals to be realised.

MESSAGE RECEIVED

If Einstein was writing a formula for communication it might look something like this Communication = Message x Audience x Effect. Or for those people that detested maths, physics, chemistry and formulas, communication is when a message moves an audience to produce an effect, either attitudinal or behavioural.

So even if there is a lot of apparent communication activity, whether it is newsletters, events, product launches, even public affairs lobbying, if there is no attempt to produce an effect in terms of adjusting the behaviour or the attitude of the audience, then there is no real communication, merely information relay.

Assertion + evidence

Take a deep breath. A message is a collection of words, actions, designs, images, sounds, non-verbal communications or some combination of these, which creates an assertion that is supported by compelling evidence, communicated in a form suitable for the intended audience.

Admittedly that sounds a bit like mumbo jumbo, or indeed the very kind of business bullshit we were advocating avoiding earlier. Perhaps an easier way of describing the message equation then, would be to look at the most common example of messaging – when we are using words to communicate. At the heart of a written or spoken message is a fact (or evidence if you prefer), plus an assertion.

So pointing at a table and saying "that is a table" is a fact, philosophical arguments, ontology and metaphysics notwithstanding. Whereas pointing at a table and saying "that is a table, and it is excellent for supporting meetings" is a message because there is an assertion capable of being contended i.e. that the table is excellent for supporting meetings. Maybe it is excellent for ping-pong, but not for holding meetings.

Failing to differentiate between plain old facts on their own and messages is one of the most common mistakes made when communicating. When we are doing face-to-face training, for example, we ask clients to send over messages that they have created in advance. Typically we will get a lot of statements of fact, with the occasional message mixed in. Usually the client is not aware of the difference.

The key in ensuring effective communications is to move from the mere relaying of facts to contending or advocating a particular value judgement based on those facts, that in turn supports your personal or organisational objective.

You can advocate that a table is great for meetings, but it is rather pointless, unless the fact is allied to some objective. If, however, you happen to be in the office furniture business then the same statement turns out to be a very good sales message, because the contention is that this is the optimum table for the particular use it has been designed for.

Note that not everything that looks like a message is a message. Lists of information are not messages but rather, as the name suggests, lists of information. A list of ingredients on the back of a packet of biscuits is not a message, for example. Slogans are a point of contention, as are images, but together with supporting material, either can serve the function of messages.

Messages behaving badly

While some people intuitively grasp the principles of good messaging, for the majority it takes practice and the help of those who have learnt what works and what does not through experience.

Unfortunately, examples of bad messages abound, from multinational marketing teams with abundant resources that should know better, and from employees just beginning to understand the power of messages in improving their performance at work and boosting their careers.

Five examples:

- Incomprehensible
- Undifferentiated
- Badly channelled – Poor channel planning, appropriateness of channel for message and vice versa
- Poorly targeted
- Passionless/inauthentic/unreal

Messages plus

Messages can be very effective used on their own, but they work best if they are used in a well thought out planned way, whether as a one off, or more likely as part of a message campaign, a managed process to achieve some overall objective.

With this in mind the following chapters in the book, after detailing the context within which messages operate in the world today and examining the constituents of a message in more detail, go on to explain how messages can be part of a broader "campaign", and the tactics and strategies that can be deployed to use messages effectively. Finally there are some tips on various practical aspects of creating and using messages.

To cut a long story short

Griot, kataribe, seanachie, bard, every country, it seems, has a name for the storyteller; the person who passes down folklore and oral history to the next generation. The subject of storytelling, may seem incongruous in a book about using messages in the 21st century, but storytelling is an art that has been refined over many centuries and has a few important lessons for people creating messages today.

While storytelling and its relevance is covered in more detail towards the end of the book, it is worth commenting briefly on the emotional component of stories.

As we have already noted messages are used within communication to change behaviours and attitudes, to produce an effect, to cause the recipients of the message to do or not do something. Messages lead the recipient to a point at which they, hopefully, make the choice that you intended them to make.

Some interesting scientific studies into the decision making process have looked at how autistic people make decisions. The research found that autistic people were perfectly capable of making a rational assessment of the data, but were still unable to make choices. Why? Individuals suffering from autism appear to have some difficulty understanding emotions, either their own or others, they are widely viewed as finding it difficult to empathise with others, for example (although this is disputed in some quarters). It seems that the differences in the emotional faculty of autistic people compared to non-autistic impacted on their ability to make choices.

Understanding the importance of the emotional content of messages and its impact is essential to creating effective messages. Emotion is not something that organisations seem to do well, or individuals, necessarily. Often the default behaviour is to have a rational reaction. The rational world is easier to quantify, easier to button down in checklists and it gives senior management comfort. This makes rational the default response in corporate communications.

So we need to draw attention to the importance of the emotions in creating messages. Also, if messages can be more effective if they are woven into a larger story, with the organisation or individual assuming the role of storyteller. It may sound like a strange, even antiquated concept, but corporate and individual storytelling can be very powerful communication tools, even in the new millennium.

GET THE MESSAGE

- A message is a collection of words, actions, designs, images, sounds, non-verbal communications or some combination of these, which creates an assertion that is supported by compelling evidence, communicated in a form suitable for the intended audience;

- Brevity is best;

- To use messages effectively you must learn how to communicate with the "so what" generation;

THE MESSAGE

- At the heart of effective messaging is a focus on the space in the mind of the audience that you want to occupy – how can you capture the mind of the message recipient;

- When it comes to using messages in the 21st century the rules of engagement have changed; you are no longer dealing with a passive audience, you are dealing with a participatory audience.

TWO

Communicating in the Connected Age

Before learning about the fundamentals of messaging is it essential to understand the context within which it takes place. Only then can we begin to create and deliver better messages.

While change is constant, we have entered a period in which a dramatic shift is taking place. One in which the way we communicate and connect is being revolutionised by technology. And just as the medium and means of communications is changing, so is the way we message.

We now live in the earliest days of the Connected Age, where everyone is, in theory at least, (and often in practice) connected to everyone else. And it is this new connectedness, which is probably the single biggest driver in changing the way that messages work, both inside enterprises, and throughout society.

Because many of us grew up in a world in which messages were, for the most part, transmitted. Messaging, whether it was via the newspapers, advertising, television or radio was largely one way.

THE MESSAGE

Sure there might have been the odd coupon to fill out and send off, you could write in to the letters column of the broadsheets, as an employee you could voice your opinions at the monthly town hall meeting, or the weekly sales meeting, as shareholder you could try to get someone to take your question at the company's annual shareholders meeting.

Usually, though the messaging was one way traffic and any interaction asynchronous. In fact, companies went out of their way to limit participation – outbound communication was limited to a select few while inbound communication was more than often channelled through formal events.

The growth of Internet marked the first phase of the revolution, with the World Wide Web and its widespread penetration of the world's households. Internetworldstats.com cited a 300% increase in Internet usage worldwide from 2000 to 2008, with 1.4 billion Internet users.

Note that the Internet is not about transmitters and receivers, but about networks, and interconnected nodes, and messaging in the Internet world reflects the interconnected nature of the net. The Internet is a giant machine for triangulating and transmitting information. The means of distribution – and information itself – has become democratised, available to anyone with access to a computer.

For the first time ever, we are shifting to a world in which messages are constantly morphing, and changing shape, based on the ability of individuals and organisations to influence opinion and dialogue.

A great example of is this is the interaction that takes place in blogging (more on web logs later in the chapter). A traditional blogger will fire up a post on their blog, and there will be a response, maybe from a company mentioned in the original blog, maybe from an individual. This response in turn elicits a response from the original blogger, and others, and so the message begins to change.

So where once, you transmitted messages, delivered them or received them, now you have to participate constantly in the creation of messages by other people, as well as your own. Companies, once exclusively in control of their message face their worst nightmare – customers and stakeholders co-creating their message with them.

However, while there is truth in the idea that neat delineations around message creation are no longer valid, that many different interested parties from customers to shareholders, from line managers, to direct reports can own, create and influence messages, regardless of where they emanate from originally, there is more to message creation than that.

This sea change doesn't diminish or alter the need for effective messaging. If anything, it necessitates that messages be created with greater rigour. Attention to honesty, transparency and co-creation are now watchwords to effective message creation where once, advertising speak, opaqueness and isolation ruled.

Growth in infrastructure

One of the main drivers underpinning the connected world is the massive growth in infrastructure around the planet. Go to places like China, and you see the impact, in the huge amounts of bandwidth they are creating, and the way people are connecting, and creating and absorbing messages. While the rest of the world has posted a 300% increase in Internet use between 2000 and 2008, in China that figure is 1000%

The growth and uptake of technology is staggering. In 2007 You Tube the video clip sharing site, which was created in 2005, consumed as much bandwidth capacity as the entire Internet did in 2000.

And there are no signs that rate of growth will slow down anytime soon. There are suggestions; for example, from firms like AT&T that within five years, just 25 homes will consume the entire capacity of the Internet of five years ago.

That is not so surprising when you think of all the different types of digital content that is flooding into these homes. We are meeting increasing numbers of people, for example, who are simply turning off the television. Or at least they are turning off their television sets. They realise that they do not need the TV set, or satellite television, or cable television.

Instead, these people can get whatever they want via the Internet. They sign up to iTunes, or other content providers, and download the programming that they want to watch – and nothing else. Not only that but they are happy to pay for it, especially when, because they are tailoring their consumption of content to fit their own preferences, it often turns out to be a cheaper way of accessing many types of content.

And not only do people get the specific content that they want, they get that content when they choose to get it. That may be some time in advance of when they would have been able to access the same content via the traditional methods. No need to wait for the news at breakfast time, or lunchtime. If you actually want to know what's happening in the rest of the world, go and look at *the New Zealand Herald* or *the Australian*, first thing in the morning. Because Australia and New Zealand have spent some time digesting and reporting the worlds' news before people in the UK or the US have even got out of their beds, so they are well ahead.

Moving targets

At the same time as billions of people are turning to the Internet for content provision, communicators are figuring out how to turn the Internet into an effective and productive communications vehicle, reaching out to the billions of people already online, and the 500,000 people who are coming online every day.

Don't make the mistake of assuming that there is a single "Internet generation," or an average Internet user, even. The Internet has been with us for over 15 years now. What was common Internet behaviour for adopters in the mid-1990s is entirely different for someone coming online for the first time in 2008, and so it will be for future users.

The people who log on for the first time in June 2008 are probably logging on, and looking at You Tube, My Space, Facebook, or some other social networks out there. Five years ago and it was more likely that a new user would look at Google. Ten years ago it would have been Yahoo and Alta Vista. Before that – Netscape Navigator, and Mosaic.

THE MESSAGE

So Internet users fasten on to You Tube. They use You Tube a lot. They spend a lot of Internet time on You Tube. And then the Next Big Thing comes along, and people begin to use You Tube slightly less, the look at You Tube every now and then, they inexorably migrate to the Next Big Thing, and then the Next Next Big Thing, and so on taking in all the new tools and tricks that come their way.

The same goes for the adoption of other new technologies. And these differences in common usage and behaviour range across gender, age groups, social groups, countries and continents.

So one of the dominant behavioural patterns that you will see in the US, for instance, is the very low use of SMS and text messaging compared to Europe. If you look at the way messages get crafted and shaped by major marketers in Europe, they are often crafting messages to conform to 120 or so characters that can fit on a mobile phone screen, and be punched out quickly.

In the US, however, communicators continue to craft deeper, email driven styles of communications. So, if you want to reach employees in Europe, for instance, with good messages, you figure out how you can text message them content.

Do not think that you can predict the way that people will use technology in the future either. It as not that long ago, after all, that a high tech future was one where every household had a home computer. Today many millions of people live in homes with multiple PCs.

Once families bought a single PC for the home, now they buy a computer for the kitchen, one for the living room, one for the bedroom, and so on. The increasing number of computers in the

Twittering

For the majority of millennials the primary mode of communication is no longer email. Instead they interact using a wide range of methods and one of those is twittering.

Why email, text or phone when you can twitter? Twittering is the latest communication craze to emerge from the birthplace of most social networking and other communication technologies – California.

If it was already hard for the world's employees to find the time to do their work with all those emails to reply to, with the advent of Twitter it has become even more difficult. A kind of micro-blogging, activity, Twitter is a service that allows people who sign up to send updates via a range of mediums - the Twitter website, instant messaging, SMS, RSS, email or through an application – that then appear on the user's profile page and are instantly sent to those people within the users permitted circle. The messages are a maximum of 140 characters long.

The website advises that the service allows people to respond to the question "What are you doing?" with useful information, such "I'm late for my meeting". Of course it hasn't taken long for organisations, political parties and anyone else out there with a message to sell to cotton on to the latest hip communication tool. Barack Obama twitters, as do film promoters.

Conceivably it could be a useful messaging medium, even a collaborative tool.

Equally likely, however, is an exchange along the lines of:
A: What are you doing?
B: I'm twittering. What are you doing?
A: I'm twittering too.

home affects the way that organisations and individuals create messages, because people experience the message in different ways depending on where they are in the house.

An adult cooking in the kitchen may use emails, instant messaging, or twitter, to find out where their children are and inform them that supper is ready. Where are the kids? What are they doing? So they are reaching out. Communicating quickly. Firing things off, and maybe watching a bit of TV while they're cooking.

In the living room, though, it is a totally different experience. The kids are using their games console to stream photos and high definition TV through the house. Totally different interconnectivity experiences in different parts of the house.

There is the same variety of user experiences at work. With the massive boom in network-connected devices, all kinds of employees are armed with fully connected, WiFi enabled devices, whether it is a BlackBerry or something else. And these devices will do just about anything, short of doing your work for you. You can use them to listen music, make phone calls, email, twitter, surf the net, take photographs, make movies, navigate your way from A to Z.

But these types of devices are just part of the connectivity mix. The consensus was that everyone in the emerging countries at least, and maybe elsewhere, will migrate to mobile devices. But, do not believe it. Go to those countries, and they are all buying PCs. Yes, they are buying mobile devices too, but they remain understandably frustrated with the mobile experience; it can be pretty hard to do certain things on a little browser window –it is not a great user experience.

Gadget fatigue soon sets in. You may even have one. New gadgets tend to be cool at first, then about three or four weeks, a month in, gadget reality sets in when you realise is a really hard way to read the newspaper after all. So out you go to get the next new gadget.

And, as the number of devices and ways of using them continues to increase, so the explosion in different types of messaging is going to continue. A good example of that is Jot, which is a comparatively new service – at the time of writing you can subscribe to the beta service online.

Jot is a great example of subscription based voice to text messaging. The idea is that it is a "to do" list. You dial the number on your phone and leave a message to call you "tomorrow morning" and it automatically knows, when you say "tomorrow morning" to assign that action to tomorrow morning. If you dial it and say, "calendar, lunch, noon, Bruce". It will put on your calendar, "lunch at noon tomorrow with Bruce".

Blogs

Blogs are another communication phenomenon in the new connected world. There is massive growth in the blogosphere. According to figures from blog search engine Technorati, as of the middle of 2008 there were some 175,000 blogs created daily, and a total of 113 million blogs, with 7.5 million of them still active. And a survey by ad agency Universal McCann estimated that 184 million bloggers were creating 570,000 posts every 24 hours.

One of the most interesting things though is that once again it is an example of people using the Internet in unexpected ways. People are not doing what the blogosphere was exclusively intended for – as a personal diary, a journaling environment. That was the original mission that people would go online, and most likely keep a personal diary.

We would all start to create and share their diaries, their comments about life. To begin with that did happen, and it still happens to some extent. To a much greater extent, however, people are using this using this online medium as their own private broadcast channels, to get across their opinions and views.

So it is a one to many kind of relationship that these people are driving, as opposed to a one to few. When they message inside these new environments, they're increasingly looking to message to many, many people.

What is also interesting is the cumulative effect of the blogosphere. People are creating more content in the blogosphere every day than all of the world's news services combined. It is the new AP, Reuters, Dow Jones, on steroids.

Look at the daily posting volumes, and it is clear that they are heavily influenced by major events, which further makes the point that these people are plugged into global news. So in other words, the original intent of the blogosphere was to record their own life, and what they are actually writing about is the life around them. It is a very different shift.

Changing behaviours

Going on a date?
New technologies such as the blog, or portable devices, don't just change the ways that society communicates, these same technologies, are fundamentally shifting the way society behaves.

Not that many of us notice it happening. We tend not to pause to reflect on our changes in behaviour. Most of us mooch along into these technologies, without much awareness of the fact that we are contributing towards major changes to some of the fundamentals of society.

A good example of this shift is online dating. It might seem trivial, but it is having a huge impact on society. One out of every eight couples married in the US last year met online. Add up the people using online dating websites Match, Yahoo! Personals, Chemistry, and eHarmony and that is a whole lot of people online and looking for love. Interestingly, commercial dating organisations have had an offline effect on messaging as well with the rise of the speed dating concept.

Speed dating encapsulates the way the world has changed over the last decade. It takes a process that might once have take weeks and compresses it into five minutes. In doing so it compresses the time available in which to make an impression. The message becomes central to the process, and to success, and new techniques are required to create an attractive, persuasive, winning message. The non-verbal messaging element is also an integral element. And of course now you can speed date online.

The online critic

Another example of the way new technology changes behaviour is the rise of the online critic. Over 60 million adults give online advice about products or services today. Advice is possibly not the best word to describe what is being provided, though. A better description might be opinions, sometimes not particularly well informed opinions, but opinions nevertheless.

Many people will have experienced the power of these messengers. Anyone who has bought, a book on Amazon, will be familiar with the customer reviews.

Scenario one: You go to Amazon to look at a book, maybe you heard about it from a friend, or read about it in a magazine. You look at the description and it seems reasonably interesting. Then you look down at the reviews, and there are lots of five star reviews. So you think, excellent it must be good and click and buy it.

Scenario two: You go to Amazon to look at a book, maybe you heard about it from a friend, or read about it in a magazine. You look at the description and it seems reasonably interesting. Then you look down at the reviews, and there are lots of negative one or two star reviews. So you think, maybe it is not so good, you don't need another book anyway, and you leave without buying it.

There is a real shift here in the power of the messenger, because suddenly the old maxim that advice that you trusted would be from reputable, informed sources, has been abandoned. Or what about that rule that you would most be willing to accept advice from close friends or family members or people like yourself.

In the case of the Amazon effect, you end up taken advice from people that you know nothing about, other than what they tell you. You have no idea who these people are. They could be incarcerated, they might never have read the book, but because they post up their views and a score, you value their opinion.

Social networks

At the same time, another interesting development is the massive, online communities that have emerged, like MySpace and Facebook, which are completely new environments in which messaging occurs.

The tendency is to still look at these groups, these messengers, through the traditional lens of target audiences. Teens. 17 to 18. Whatever.

But that is not how it works. These are very amorphous masses of people that are communicating and messaging all day long, on a lot of irreverent, irrelevant, disconnected information. If you just spend an hour or so on Facebook, managing your Facebook account, the experience can be completely unpredictable.

One of the things that makes Facebook and these similar applications so attractive to us as humans is the irreverent, surprising way that they work. You go on to Facebook, and someone will have left something on your fun wall that you don't even know about, or think about. Someone that you only ever had sort of a passing but friendly relationship with will posted amazing photos from their weekend in Paris, someone else has written a poem. Your network of friends comes alive for you, right, in a very virtual way.

So this is a very different world. If MySpace was a country, as of 2008 it would be the fourth largest country in the world, between the US and Indonesia and the USA. And on its current steep trajectory and velocity there is a very good chance that MySpace will soon be equivalent to the largest country in the world in terms of population size,

What does this all tell us? Why is it important? It tells us that in terms of message creation and distribution, a lot of the traditional notions that we once held to be true, and really important to us, actually carry no weight at all in this new connected world. These new messengers are seriously changing our view of the world.

THREE

The Anatomy of a Message

So what are the different elements that make up a message? It is difficult to construct a successful, effective message without first understanding what makes messages tick. Take a message apart and you discover what makes it work really well. The value in doing this is that it allows you to diagnose messages, to identify what elements need fixing in order to improve a message; it makes it easier to refine, fine-tune, and tune-up messages.

First though, before looking at the anatomy of a message, there are a number of things to note.

Allied to a cause

As noted in Chapter One, the rule of thumb is that a message is a fact plus a value. A message has something that is verifiable – a fact – plus something of value to us – else why bother, and we call that the cause.

So before you can have a message you need a cause or a purpose.

THE MESSAGE

The function of the message is to help a person or organisation realise a cause; to help them achieve a defined aim. So, for example, if you are concerned about the world's ecosystem and are campaigning to get people to save the world's seas, then one way of achieving this, is by using focused messages as part of the campaign to help realise your cause, and try to get people to buy into your proposition that the seas need to be saved.

Of course your cause doesn't have to be about as noble as saving the seas. It can be slightly more selfish in motive; making a good sales presentation, for example. But, whatever it is that you want to achieve, you will want to enlist other people to help you achieve it, and so you need to tell them what it is that you want them to do, and how to do it. That is where the message is comes in.

And, although we do not want to get too philosophical here, a message is more than just an idea. Ideas are involved, but they are only part of the story. You can have an idea, but if you want to get it across, if you want to communicate that idea, you can do that best as a message.

For the communicator it is worth noting that although an appropriate use for messaging is to represent your cause, that cause does not need to be popular. Sure, you can have a cause to increase sales, or save the whales. But, you can also have a cause to do less popular things, whether it is to cut costs or build more nuclear power stations.

Why do some messages work?

For messages to be successful, they need to demonstrate certain characteristics.

THE ANATOMY OF A MESSAGE

Although the anatomy of a message is mainly about burrowing into the message and considering the internal aspects, the external context is also important; messages have to be both timed appropriately and apposite.

Take President John F Kennedy's "Special Message to the Congress on Urgent National Needs," made on May 25, 1961. Aiming high, President Kennedy told Congress, "I believe that this nation should commit itself to achieving the goal, before this decade is out, of landing a man on the moon and returning him safely to the earth."

While this message was well constructed, it was also set in the right context to win over the hearts and minds of its audience and galvanise America into action.

America was engaged in a battle of ideologies and technologies with Russia, and Kennedy makes the most of this political backdrop in persuading his audience to action.

"Finally," he says, "if we are to win the battle that is now going on around the world between freedom and tyranny, the dramatic achievements in space which occurred in recent weeks should have made clear to us all, as did the Sputnik in 1957, the impact of this adventure on the minds of men everywhere, who are attempting to make a determination of which road they should take."

So the context for the message was America in competition with the USSR. The message was also given at a time when America needed to reassert its pride following the Bay of Pigs fiasco, the unsuccessful attempt by US backed Cuban exiles to invade Cuba and overthrow Fidel Castro.

Importantly, it was also a time when Kennedy's goal of putting a man on the moon was achievable from a technological standpoint. There would have been little point for a previous US President to make a similar appeal as such a feat would not have been technically feasible and would have appeared implausible, undermining the power of the message.

In other words, going back to the fact plus value part of the equation, the message needs to be verifiable, otherwise it is, certainly in this example, just science-fiction.

Authenticity matters

Messages need to be authentic. You cannot use a message to motivate someone to behave in a certain way, if the recipient of the message does not trust and believe the message giver. Consequently, if a message is not verifiable, if it cannot be checked out, or, if the context fails to support the message, then the message will appear inauthentic. It will fail to do its job.

The issue of authenticity is increasingly important in a world where verification can be obtained almost instantaneously, at the click of a mouse.

In January 2007, for example, after complaints about the poor condition of Army housing stock, UK government minister Derek Twigg made a statement about the government's expenditure on improving Army accommodation. The statement was intended to reassure and persuade the public that the government was dealing with the situation.

THE ANATOMY OF A MESSAGE

Twenty years ago and that statement might not have been forthcoming. In 2007, however, the Internet and the ease of modern communications meant that the families of military personnel were able to bring their living conditions to the attention of the world's media. Hundreds of people living in Army accommodation were posting comments and pictures on the Internet that highlighted the problems in a way that would simply not have been possible until recently.

In a world where there are millions of bloggers armed with digi-cams, cameras, and sound recorders, if you fail to represent things as they really are, you will be found out. In today's world, with the ubiquitous ability to photograph events, it is easy to debunk misrepresentations and half-truths.

This is something that Hillary Clinton found out to her personal cost, when she discovered how easy it is to debunk a message, while on the campaign trail for the Democratic Party's nomination for US President.

Clinton was filmed on camera describing a visit to Bosnia in which she recalled getting off of the aircraft, putting her head down and running to the transport vehicles, without any greeting ceremony, to evade sniper fire.

Unfortunately for Clinton, it was not long before a clip of her trip was being aired on national television showing Clinton, the first lady, and her daughter casually strolling through a large greeting party, not wearing a helmet, and even having time to stop and talk to a young Bosnian girl. In explaining the discrepancy between Clinton's recollections and actual events, a spokesperson for the

Clinton camp used the unfortunate term "misspoke", as did Clinton herself, which only added to the sense of dissembling.

Hillary Clinton is not the only politician to appear inauthentic after a run-in with the cameras. Back in 1974, President Richard M. Nixon was pictured en route to the Royal Palace in Brussels to have lunch with Belgium's King Baudouin. The black and white photo by Associated Press photographer Charles Tasnadi shows Nixon, arm outstretched, shaking hands with a bystander, while checking his watch, seemingly oblivious to the well wisher.

Some years later George Bush was caught on camera checking his wristwatch in the middle of a 1992 televised presidential debate with Bill Clinton and Ross Perot. At the time the candidates were supposed to be responding to a question from a member of the audience about how the recession had affected the candidates. By looking at his watch, an apparently bored and impatient Bush sent out all the wrong messages.

So where once the main means of debunking a message was the written word, today it is much more likely to be the visual image; an executive makes a claim about something, but the visual image tells a different story.

Messages are not wallpaper

Given that authenticity is important, it should be obvious that messages cannot and should not be used to paper over the cracks in the corporate edifice caused by poor practices.

Messaging may be related to the practice of public relations, which

THE ANATOMY OF A MESSAGE

Message memo: Reputational baggage

When Terminal 5 was opened at Heathrow Airport on March 17, 2008, British Airways and BAA seemed sure that the brand new £4.3 billion terminal was ready for action. That much was clear from an earlier media conference in which at least one BA executive expressed that they were confident that the terminal and its new state of the art baggage handling system would be operationally ready on the day.

In the event such confidence turned out to be misplaced as the baggage handling process went completely awry with unfortunate consequences for BA's reputation. Perhaps, however, worse than the chaos caused by opening day teething problems, in which hundreds of flights were cancelled and thousands of bags piled up or went missing, was the way that BA handled those problems.

BA was not particularly quick to provide information to customers and seemed to, momentarily at least, be in a state of denial. At one point executives appeared to flee from journalists refusing to take questions.

Where was CEO, Willie Walsh? He most obviously was not down on the floor, shirt sleeves rolled up, acknowledging the problems, helping out with the baggage, and generally pitching in. And while he later took it on the chin in terms of blame – although other senior executives lost their jobs, the collective message sent out by BA's reaction to events on that first day was a not a good one for its reputation.

THE MESSAGE

is quite often associated with the art of dissimulation – concealing the truth – but messages are not spin; they are not cover for various behaviours or decisions.

Take the following extract from a January 2008 corporate communication by Shell, the multinational energy giant.

> *"Despite a good track record and performance, the IT function recognised that meeting these increasing demands in terms of scale, improved productivity and better connectivity, requires a step change in IT delivery.*
>
> *With the new IT Infrastructure delivery model, services and control points that are strategic to Shell, are retained where as most of the service delivery will be provided by external suppliers. In short, IT will outsource delivery but maintain control. As a result a significant number of staff, currently employed by IT Infrastructure will be transferred to the new suppliers. The outsourced IT Infrastructure staff will continue to support Shell and the experience and knowledge they bring to their new employers is highly valuable."*

Although not immediately obvious, examine the corporate speak more closely, and it becomes clear that "a step change in IT delivery" means a lot of IT people will be losing their jobs at Shell, being transferred instead to an outsourcing provider. Dressing the message up in such convoluted language just makes it seem as if Shell is trying to downplay and minimise what is happening.

A better message from Shell would have been one that was much shorter, in plain English (see Box), that had some personality, and that adhered to the pointers in this book.

> **Message memo: Corporate bullshit stinks**
>
> A piece by Gene Weingarten in the Washington Post in 2007, titled Read it and Lacrimate, drew attention to the proliferation of corporate bullshit that often passes for messages these days.
>
> In this instance, Weingarten used some press releases to illustrate his point. In one, from MasterCard, the release announced "an incremental change in one of its programs so as to maximise 'categories of spend' by 'scoring cardholder activity against specific parameters using a rules-based engine.'
>
> Another release had HQ Sustainable Maritime Industries Inc. identifying itself as "a leader in toxin-free integrated aquaculture and aquatic product processing" that "practices cooperative sustainable aquaculture, using nutraceutically enriched feeds."

So, before considering the anatomy of the message in more detail it is worth reaffirming that the function of good messaging is to recruit people to your cause. The cause does not need to be popular, but it does have to be authentic to be successful.

The anatomy of the message

A message is made up from a number of discrete elements: the *active ingredient*, the *behavioural change* and *the example*.

Element one: The active ingredient

The active ingredient really is the part of the message that does the job. Look at the back of a packet of any soap powder detergent and you'll somewhere on it "phosphate or zyolyte equals x%". That is the bit that does the cleaning. The rest are just bulking agents, perfumes, stuff that makes the product good for home cleaning. The bit that does the cleaning is the active ingredient.

When you are scanning a message, you have to run a verbal highlighter over it; you are looking for the bits that are the active ingredient, in order to discriminate the part that does the messaging. You put on your x-ray spectacles, take a look at the message, and should be able to identify the bit that is really powerful.

On June 8, 1972, a number of Vietnamese families ran from the village of Trang Bang, along Route-1, their bodies burned by napalm. Associated Press photographer Huynh Cong Ut, captured the moment with an iconic snapshot of Phan Thi Kim Phuc, a young girl screaming from the pain of her third degree burns. (Phan, who was just nine at the time, survived)

It was terrifying moment for Phan. It was also a difficult moment for Dow Chemicals, the company that made the Napalm that caused her injuries. That photo, the visual image of that young burning girl running towards the camera, reinforced the company's association with death.

Dow, together with the US Air Force, invented napalm-b in 1965. Only a year later and students, right across America's college and university campuses, armed with placards bearing the simple message, "Dow kills", began demonstrating against Dow. Soon Dow recruiters visiting campuses were having to escape angry mobs by climbing through windows, or being blockaded on campus for hours.

In May 1968 students marched on Dow's US located global HQ, and

THE ANATOMY OF A MESSAGE

in 1969 disrupted the annual shareholder meeting. By this time others were joining the protests. The stock price took a hit. Chairman Carl Gerstacker acknowledged that the affair was hurting the company.

In November 1969 Dow announced it was ceasing production of napalm for the US government. But by now the damage to Dow's reputation was done. Dow had developed the comma problem, that inevitable pause after mentioning a company's name and before associating it with something negative. Enron, the troubled energy company. Bear Stearns, the troubled investment bank. Because of the bad press over the use of napalm in the Vietnam War, Dow became inextricably associated with the manufacture of napalm, and the death, destruction and suffering that the chemical caused.

While the association impacted on a number of areas of Dow's business, one of the most important was recruitment. At the time, President Herbert Doan said that he was concerned that the protests were costing Dow the creative minds that might invent "the next great thing."

So once Dow had committed to a decision to stop manufacturing napalm for the US government how could it go about rescuing its reputation?

Part of the answer was by using clever, effective messaging, and as part of that a strong active ingredient. Take the example below, an excerpt from a transcript of a Gerstacker interview:

> *Gerstacker: We don't make Napalm. I'd rather talk about products we do make. Dow is in the life science business, for example we have a measles vaccine that's been out since 1965.*

THE MESSAGE

About fifty million US children have been vaccinated, I think the key thing here again is that there are five thousand children in the US today who are not mentally retarded, and all that anguish in all those years because of this measles vaccine.

This is great use of messaging. For a start, it is short, punchy, succinct and motivational. The tendency to over elaborate is avoided. Messages should not go on for paragraphs and paragraphs in the hope that if enough mud is thrown at the wall some is bound to stick. The perfect message would be even shorter, down to around fifteen words or so; a couple of short sentences. But perfection is never easy to achieve.

The other brilliant thing about Dow's use of the message here is the all important active ingredient. The key message in the passage is, "Dow is in the life-science business." The active ingredient is "life science". "Life science" means not "death science". By using the word "life" in this phrase, Gerstacker directly counters the association of Dow with napalm, the Vietnam War and the photo of the girl on the road. In a very clever and succinct way Gerstacker is saying that Dow Chemical is about a life affirming future, rather than about a negative destructive historical past and the firm's involvement in Vietnam. It is a very powerful message.

Still relevant
While Dow was facing its recruitment challenge over 25 years ago, the Dow example is just as relevant for organisations today in terms of messaging. The shortage of talent is a significant issue for organisations operating in today's global; economy. MBAs from top business schools, for example, are deluged with offers, perhaps more than ever they can afford to be choosy about who they work

for. Consequently corporate reputation and employer branding plays a key factor in attracting talent.

At the same time the new generation of employers, the millennial generation, and their successors, are a fussy lot. Salary and benefits are just part of the mix of factors that persuade this generation to work for one firm or another. Other factors like corporate culture and corporate social responsibility become more important. For example, for a potential hire choosing between BP, Exxon, or Shell, the decision may come down to the social responsibility values that each company espouses.

Communication is a relational concept, you don't communicate within a vacuum; there is always an implied other. Every time an individual or organisation makes a communication, the message it gives out is received by an audience. Organisations and individuals must, therefore always have in mind the possible audiences, whenever they are communicating with others. And this is as true for the individual talking about their organisation in a bar after work, as it is with a company and its annual report.

So it pays to have your virtual audience in the room with you, potential recruits, for example, as you develop and construct a message, including its active ingredient.

What makes a successful active ingredient?
Perhaps the most important factor in arriving at the right active ingredient is its appropriateness, given the overall intention of the message. Good active ingredients are relevant to the audience and the message giver.

Note that you need to be relevant to both sides, not just the end audience. The active ingredient has to match the message givers agenda. It should not be just something they want to be associated with. Careful consideration must be given to overall goals. An oil company might want to be associated with "green" activity, but ultimately if that association and the behavioural change brought about by the message is going to hit their operations, then they may need to avoid that association.

The active ingredient should stretch a cause as well, pushing it beyond the average. Dow Chemical's active ingredient "life science" addressed the core cause, to get people wanting to work for the company again, and it also pushed the boundaries, switching from an association with death, destruction and the past – to affirmation of life.

Element two: Behavioural change
Messages exist to do a job. They are there to convert, not, as with the many millions of pointless emails that ricochet around the electronic ether, For Your Information. There is far too much FYI going on in the world today, too much Cc, Bcc, and Forward mail.

Avoid the Cc syndrome where we copy in people for reasons other than elucidating a point, usually for political reasons to show someone that we are very busy, to create a paper trail in case we need to produce evidence at a later date, to shift responsibility to other people.

Avoid indiscriminate informational relay, and so avoid contributing to the information overload we all face in our everyday life. What we need to do is discriminate. Messages should be discriminatory; they discriminate from all the bullshit and unnecessary verbiage.

Messages say what we really want to say, and do that in way that changes attitudes and behaviour. Take the message: London Business School is *the* international business school.

London Business School (LBS) is in competition with a number of other leading business schools around the world, notably those in the US, such as Harvard, Wharton, Stanford, and MIT Sloan. On a strict head to head basis LBS might struggle to stand out against its competitors. So it uses its message to reframe the debate in its favour.

US business schools are well known for having a comparatively low percentage of international students compared to European schools. "International" is the active ingredient. The message attempts to persuade prospective MBA students that a good business education has to be international. And that means attending a school with a broad international mix of students; LBS rather than a US school.

Going back to Dow Chemical, it was clearly in a controversial industry at the time and one of the operational difficulties it faced was gaining and retaining top recruits. So in this context, recruits were a primary audience. The object of the Dow message was to say to recruits: "Come and think about building your career with us again, come and have your working future with us, because we are about positive, future thinking". And all without reaffirming the negativity from which Gerstacker was trying to extricate Dow.

Often messages make the mistake of settling for platitudes, instead of an active ingredient that will persuade people to change behaviours or attitudes. Political messages, which are frequently designed down to the lowest common denominator, to be as inoffensive as possible to the entire audience, are a common example of this type of message.

THE MESSAGE

Take a political message, such as: "We need to have safer streets for our children". Here, "safe" and "children" are the active ingredients.

But a message like this that is not going to convert anybody. What does it say that isn't self-evident? We know this already. Instead, tell us something that is really going to stimulate us. Do not just offer platitudes.

A good way of checking the salience of messaging, is to try and work out if anybody would ever say the opposite? Would anybody actually say: "We do not need safer streets for our children". If you can't automatically form an opposite position to that which you are presenting, then you are probably not saying anything that is particularly engaging.

So messages are not about consensus, but about converting. Politicians are great at going for consensus. Messages are really for converting, looking for people with similar views, and trying to bring them onto your platform.

Look at your message. Does it have a powerful driver – like "life-science" or "international" – that is relevant and matches your agenda? Will it actually convert behaviours? Or will it instead, get the opposite response -"so what"? Because, as we discussed in Chapter One, "so what" is the current zeitgeist. Everything is "so what", or in more common parlance – "I don't care".

The message has to be that the audience should care.

Element three: Example
Most people, nervous speech makers especially, have a tendency to say too much (too quickly), they tend to embroider their points, they

THE ANATOMY OF A MESSAGE

cite an anecdote, or quote a piece of data, and they deduce a conclusion.

Messaging asks you to reverse what might be considered the more normal and natural process by starting with your conclusion. First comes the overall point you are trying to make, followed by the example, the anecdotes, or the data. The conclusion leads; the evidence is consigned to a supporting role.

Automatically that inversion gives you control. Control is one of the bywords of all good communication. You control the message, you control the channel, and you control the audience.

The way you go about that is first in the structuring of the content of the message. Start with your topline conclusion first, and then drop down to the example, or the detail, that supports or verifies that conclusion.

If you are going to make a contention, you will want to verify it, and when you verify, that verification must relate to the active ingredient. So for Dow, when Gerstacker talks about life-sciences, he backs it up with: "for example, we have a measles vaccine that's been out since 1965."

In some ways it is like being in the court of law. You are the lawyer for the defence. You contend that you client is innocent, and then produce evidence to support your claims.

Remember also that the aim is to illustrate or verify the main contention, not necessarily to scientifically prove it. It is very easy to become obsessed with the idea of proof, but a scientific standard of proof is not necessary in the world of communication.

If anything, the science community aptly demonstrates the limited value of scientific proof. If you take most science related issues, whether it is climate change or nuclear power, there will be brilliant experts on both sides of the argument passionately convinced that they are right – and the other side is wrong. Not only that, but "the experts" will produce reams of data to support their view.

Too much data is often confusing, so while veracity and evidence is important, you must be careful to use the evidence in a way that supports your contention and its plausibility, credibility, and authenticity, rather than muddying the waters with data overload.

Consistency counts

Once you understand the composition of messages, the next step is the practical construction of the message, more of which in the next chapter. A couple of final points, however, before moving on to the practical how-to.

As mentioned before messages need to be shorter rather than longer, they need to be short and focused. But they also need to be few, rather than many and more varied. Because the more varied your messages are, the less likely they are to be consistent, and the less consistency there is, the less credible the message giver appears.

If you say a few things continually, you are more likely to be impactful, than if you say many things in a variety of fashions, some good and some average. If there are too many messages, people will complain that they don't know what a person or organisation stands for any more. People distrust messages that are continually emerging, and changing.

THE ANATOMY OF A MESSAGE

When Microsoft, the computing giant, started business, its overriding message was, "a computer on every desk and in every home." Over the next twenty five years that simple, short, powerful, message, left no one in any doubt what Microsoft's vision was as it became one of the most successful companies of all time.

Also, organisations and individuals often view messaging as an exercise in rhetoric. Consequently they labour for much longer than they need to in an attempt to find the perfect words for their message. However, the reality is that while the words, and in some cases even the order of the words, are important, it essential not to lose sight of the essence of the message and its objectives.

Sure, you need to work out what the active ingredients are, because they are your drivers, but after that, you can often afford to be reasonably relaxed about the phrasing of the messaging itself.

The active ingredient, the structure, and the relevance, of the message, and that it is focused and short where possible, these are critical to the success of the message. Ironically, however, the words, or the order of the words at least should always be subservient to the meaning.

So do not allow the words to obscure the need for a clear active ingredient, clear behavioural change for the end audience that you are trying to convert, and powerful and focused examples.

GET THE MESSAGE

- Messages need to be allied to a cause;

THE MESSAGE

- Although the anatomy of a message is mainly about burrowing into the message and considering the internal aspects, the external context is also important; messages have to be both timed appropriately and apposite.

- Messages need to be authentic;

- Messages are not wallpaper;

- Three essential elements of messages are: the active ingredient; behavioural change; and the example.

- If you want to be credible, your messages need to be consistent.

FOUR

Time to Deliver

People quite often see messaging as synonymous with glossy annual reports, or press releases for corporate social responsibility projects, but messages are functioning ingredients, not just things to be laminated and stuck up on the wall. Messages are active rather than passive; they are really there to do a job for the individual, or for the business.

This chapter takes a more functional, rather than theoretical, approach to the issue of messaging. It is about tactical planning, in other words planning a particular event or act of communication, whether it is for a media interview, a customer presentation, an annual report, an address of some kind, even a best man's speech. It should cover people for any act of delivering a message in "public", and that doesn't have to mean outside the organisation,.

Tactical planning should be distinguished from strategic planning, which is more about dealing with issues such as: how can I communicate my short, medium, long-term, objectives? How can I sensitise my message to differing sets of audiences, from customers through to government public policy, and non-government organisations, employees, the financial community? How do I get different people in the organisation to speak to differing subjects, but in concert, or in harmony.

Lost in the details

When delivering a message people tend to make a number of common mistakes.

To begin with many people make the mistake of over embroidering their points, they deliver the message in tortuous detail losing the audience in the process.

There is tendency within organisations, for example, to think that the person who is the biggest expert on a particular subject, is also going to be a great communicator. However, while it is understandable to want people who are knowledgeable on a subject to talk about it, people who are brilliant at what they do, whether they are a research chemist, a financial analyst or a supply chain manager should not be assumed to be brilliant communicators.

If you go into the finance department of business schools and talk to somebody who is brilliant at derivatives or decision sciences, ask them what it is that they do, and more often than not they will lose you very quickly.

When people get lost in the detail, it is for a number of reasons. First, it is because they are comfortable talking or writing about what they know, and the more detail, they think, the better they are relating the material to others. Secondly, they are unable to discriminate between what is important and what is not important in terms of the message.

So it is important to take a step back and consider what the message is that you are conveying, and then try to top line your points, streamline them, getting rid of excess detail so that you do not obscure the main message. Otherwise a lot of people are going to get confused and then mentally switch off. Remember to focus on your cause and the audience, rather than focus on the minutiae of the content.

One professor that we were helping, for example, complained about getting nervous before presentations, and also wanted to improve his effectiveness. The problem was that this person saw these occasions, as moments for self aggrandisement, as moments of personal fame. So that was both a reason why he felt nervous, he was focusing on himself rather than the audience, and also why he was less effective than he could have been – his criterion for success was whether people congratulated him afterwards rather than whether people acted on his message.

In fact the professor's presentations were very poor, judged on the basis of whether they engaged people in his cause. There were too many details, too many slides, rather than speaking to people. The presentation went on far too long. It was unstructured. Much of the presentation seemed to be an attempt to establish credentials and justify why people had come to see him, when he was unquestionably a leading expert on the particular subject area, and so did not need to do that.

The Message Card

The message card is a tool designed to help focus and organise your thoughts for a particular event. Ordering key messages is crucial to their effectiveness, and to enable you to gain control of the interaction between you and your message and the audience.

Filling in the card allows you to inhale content, personalise content, and therefore be more authentic and focused when you deliver it. It is a packaging process but in a profound sense; normally packaging is seen as a cosmetic exercise, where you put a nice wrapper over something. But the packaging process here is an internalisation process, where you are actually engaging with the content at a personal level, before you speak it out again. So you are immersing yourself in the content by filling in the card.

Do not think that you are producing just an aide memoir, which is what you will have at the end, but by you filling it out yourself, rather than getting someone else to do it, you are getting to grips with the material yourself, you are getting ready for that act of communication. We have seen examples of senior executives getting other people to fill the card in for them, but when this happens the final message just comes across as an exercise in passing along the received view of someone else; it is just not good enough.

So this is the moment where you need to struggle a little bit and struggling is good when you are filling in the card. Because first of all you realise that it is actually not that easy a thing to do. And by struggling you will add rigour to your journey. It makes you think about whether you really need to say certain things. There is not much space on the card so you need to be focused, relevant, and timely, and also ensure that your message does a job by converting people. So in many ways what the message card does is to focus you on cutting out the bull.

TIME TO DELIVER

The Message Card

Context Message: *What's the unmet need?*

Example: *Use a statistical / analytic example*

News-Hook Message: *What's the new event or announcement?*

Example: *Use a concrete / vivid example*

Call-to-Action Message: *What are the implications?*

Example: *Use a case-study or story / anecdote*

Three messages

The main part of the message card task is about selecting three messages: the context message; the news hook message; and the call to action message.

The context message

When you are talking to a stakeholder in a business situation, whether it is a customer, shareholders, even members of the local community, the temptation is to move straight to the subject of the presentation, whether it is a new product, or a corporate announcement.

However, even if you are pressed on a breaking news story that relates to your organisation, or quizzed regarding other contemporary events, take your time and resist answering news related questions, step back a little, start off with a message that puts your information in proper *context*. This generally means providing

THE MESSAGE

a sense of perspective on the news story – by giving historical background or trend information, relating your information to an accepted view and so on.

This will allow you to establish authority and take more control. It also allows you to present your point in a way that makes most sense from the organisation's perspective, providing you with an opportunity to influence how the rest of the presentation or interview plays out.

News hook message

Having set out the context, which looks back to the past, next comes the news hook message which deals with the here and now. Because communication has to be action-orientated, you have to move your audience on from the present, closer to the point where you realise your business goal. News-hook messages are "launch" messages – dealing directly with the topic under review and explaining the significance of the event.

Remember, it is important to provide a sense of action and purpose that moves the audience along from the background to present day. The news hook should be something that will generate interest among the audience, such as an announcement, a new product launch, significant news about our business, or in the case of a media event, for example, a necessary response to an issue that is being covered in the media at that time. The news hook should also support the organisation's goals.

The news hook does not convert an objective into action on its own, however, a third message is needed which must be forward-looking. This should give the audience something to think about or do.

Call to action message

The third message must be forward-looking and give the audience something to think about or lead to a change in behaviour. A call-to-action message is typically focused on the future and embedded within it is the change you want your audience to make after they have heard what you have to say. It evaluates the subject of the news hook message, and moves audiences towards your proposition.

The three message system

The context, news hook and call-to-action messages work very well, they support and lead on from each other. Try the following as an exercise. Print off a message card and fill it out. Select a topic to be the subject of your discussion, and keep in mind the audience to whom you want to get your messages across. Fill in the message card using the system we describe earlier. Just the messages for now – the examples can be completed at a later point.

SUPPORTING A MESSAGE: EVIDENCE TO ILLUSTRATE THE CASE IN POINT

Supporting a message

In the infomania age, with attention spans decreasing rapidly, people are much less willing to give up their valuable time to listen to messages. In what is fast becoming a world of sound bites, the normal methods of communication are being turned on their head. Instead of telling a story and letting the audience work out the meaning and purpose for themselves, you need to start with the

THE MESSAGE

conclusion, get to the point quickly, and then do the "how and why" afterwards.

This second element, the support or validation of the message, is still an essential part of messaging, however. It is the part where you become an advocate for your message. Good communicators are passionate advocates for their case, and able to contend a point that is clear and supportive.

It is important to note that the output of messaging is clarity and understanding, but not necessarily agreement. Quite often people become desperate to gain agreement as a result of their communication, and will even water down the message in order to do this. But agreement is not something you can control.

To help manage expectations, you need to bear in this mind. If communication breaks down, or employees or stakeholders disagree with each other, it will usually be based on confusion and misperception. So focus on things you can control. Make your contentions and support or validate them through the examples you select. Ensure that people understand you and are clear about your perspective. This is as much as you can hope for; if people agree and act as you want then it is a bonus. If you can clear up misunderstandings through good communication you have made progress.

The message triangle

We have already mentioned that each example needs to validate the message. But think of that function as only one corner of a triangle – it has two more criteria to fulfil.

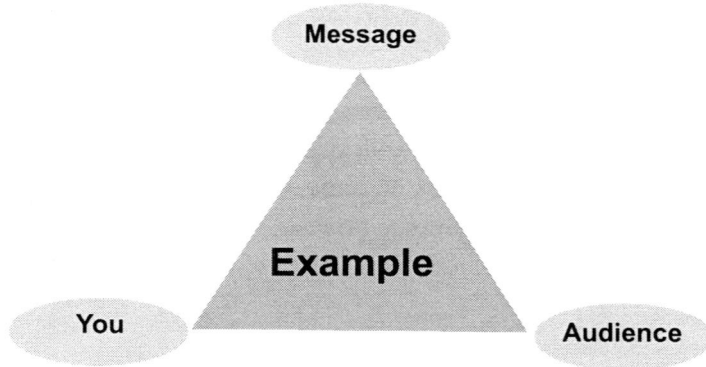

Figure 1 The message triangle

The audience
The example must also connect or be relevant to the audience. This will provide you with a way to localise a corporate generic message – by using an example which is sensitive to the needs of the particular audience.

If you have an example of your business being a leader in innovation, which you are communicating to an audience in Argentina, then you should use an example of innovation in action in Argentina.

That audience will be much more interested in hearing local stories

– and you can use examples to connect general and trans-national messages to local audiences. Of course you can sensitise examples by job function rather than geography. So if you were using the innovation message to a trade or business-to-business audience – you could use examples of innovation within your companies' supply chain. The same applies in terms of sensitising messages to the audience when delivering a personal message.

This provides you with a way to localise what might be a generic message. Remember, if communication is an information transaction, then the currency you use is credibility. There is little point in being word perfect, if your credibility is low or non-existent. For you to be convincing you need to buy into the message yourself.

You
Finally, as well as having the right supporting evidence to validate and support your messages, and connecting the message with the audience you also need to make a personal connection the person the message.

It is one thing to give a message, but another to do it convincingly. To be convincing you need to be passionate, credible, even inspiring, and the practical aspects of this are covered in more detail in later chapters.

Bear in mind too, that unlike personal messages, organisational messages are usually kicked around, edited and re-edited, and finally agreed upon by many constituent elements within the organisation.

If a camel is a horse designed by committee, messages often end up as the corporate communication equivalent. Examples, however, allow more opportunity for self-expression, tending not to be so centrally controlled by the organisation.

As the communicator you can select the examples to illustrate your messages, and make sure that you choose examples that you feel personally passionate about. By doing this it will even allow you to sell messages that you may not be personally energised about.

Two types of example

Two types of examples are particularly useful: *data* and *hearts-and-minds*. People in organisations and corporations tend to be very happy talking about data.

Imagine, for example, you are travelling into London for a conference on transport systems in the world's cities, and you are late getting to the venue.

You could deliver the message, for example, that London's transport system is falling apart, that is your assertion, with the words "falling apart" being the active ingredient. Then you could back this up with the fact that the average speed of cars in London today is 12 miles an hour, slower than it used to be in Victorian times.

This is a data example which connects with the audience, as it is about London where the presentation is taking place, and with you, because it relates to why you are late and your frustrations with the transport system. It also helps to reinforce your credentials in terms of knowledge about city transport.

THE MESSAGE

Alternatively, you could give an example of how your baggage was lost on you flight, you got held up in Heathrow, the connecting trains were suffering major delays because of engineering works, you had trouble getting a taxi and when you did, the traffic was snarled up all the way from the outskirts of London into the centre.

This last scenario is the hearts and minds example. It is your personal scenario, still supporting the same message, but providing you with a personal connection rather than the rational authority of the data example.

Both the data and hearts and minds examples have a role to play. One gives you authority; the other gives you the personal connection. Data is more analytical, and rational, appealing to the logical mind, whereas hearts and minds is more of an emotional connect. Gerstacker had a bias towards the data example. He validated his contentions about Dow using a statistic – 5,000 US children alive that wouldn't be if it were not for the work of Dow Chemical.

So you have at your disposal, as you go through the message card, the ability to use both data and hearts and minds examples. You will find that for your context message that it is much better to have a data example, as you want to be crisp and authoritative,

For your call to action messages, though, it is better to use a hearts and minds example, because you are trying to convert people to your cause, and hearts and minds examples have emotional connect.

When people make decisions, they think that they are making them as rational decisions, but often they are making them based on emotions, they are responding to the emotions that they feel at a particular time, or that are aroused by a particular message. The hearts and minds example gives you the emotional reason to believe.

> **Message memo: All encompassing**
>
> When we use messaging we are battling for a share of the space in people's minds. A message is only useful in so far as it is acknowledged and retained. While we may be inundated with thousands of messages everyday we tend not to come after a day's work complaining that we just cannot stand the information overload. That is because, for the most part, all these messages wash over us. We get used to blocking out the external world.
>
> Consequently the average person looks without seeing, listens without hearing, touches without feeling, eats without tasting, moves without physical awareness, inhales without awareness of odour or fragrance, and talks without thinking.
>
> If you don't think that's you try taking a pen and piece of paper and noting down all your sensory experience over the next 15 minutes. Pay deliberate attention to the world around you during the day. You will be surprised at how much more you notice.
>
> Take a look at the environments of different retailers. If you work in an office, or a discrete workspace, pay attention to the details. Is it messy? What is on the walls? What can you smell? What can you hear?

> So, one of the things you have to start doing if you are creating messages, is to think about the environment in which those messages are being delivered.
>
> If, for example, you are communicating a message about being innovative and smart, you are not going to successfully compete for mind space if the office space with its uniform grey office cubicles and drab wallpaper, screams dull and ordinary, or the website is a stock out of a box plain vanilla website. You will struggle to convince people what a creative influence you are, if you pitch up looking like an accountant with the regulation suit and tie.

Under pressure

When you are delivering a message in person, it is not always easy to stick to the message, especially when you are under pressure. If you are dealing with the media, for example, they can ask awkward distracting questions designed to knock you off course. Before you know it you are way off message.

It is the same when you are interacting with other stakeholders, whether it is customers or internal business units. People do not always want to listen to the entire story that you have to tell them, they may not even care to listen to a small part of it.

In general discussion, or conversation, the Satellite Response System (SRS) is a way of keeping your credibility at the same time as deploying your messages.

The idea is to break down the interaction into three parts – the question, the issue, and the message. With a bit of focus and skill it is possible to turn even seemingly unrelated questions or conversation into messaging opportunities.

So take an example where someone wants to get across the message that: "We are pioneers in innovation", but the question that is directed at them is "How many employees have you got?"

The immediate and most obvious response is "We have about x employees". That is a good answer, in that it is accurate and it answers the question. Unfortunately, it is a poor answer in terms of the message, because it doesn't make any point related to the innovation message at all.

So the less immediate, less obvious, but more effective response is "We've got x people working for us which represents a substantial growth over the last 10 years. This growth is necessary because of our increased focus on innovation".

In this version of the answer the person bridges to an issue that relates to the message by using the original question. So via employee numbers, and then growth, there is enough room for manoeuvre to bridge to the message of innovation.

This method also allows the person answering the question, or engaged in discussion, to remain credible with the audience, as the original question is still answered, while at the same time gracefully shifting to the message. It is a quid pro quo, the person asking a question, gets the answer they want, and you get to deliver your message. Remember that what you want to avoid is appearing evasive, as this undermines credibility.

So the trick is to deal with the subject introduced, but at the same time not get fixated by it. Also remember that in discussion, Q&A, and conversation situations, you cannot afford to just sit back and wait for convenient cues for your key messages, as they may never arise. So, sometimes you have to force the issue.

GET THE MESSAGE

- The message card is a tool designed to help focus and organise your thoughts for a particular event. Ordering key messages is crucial to their effectiveness, and to enable you to gain control of the interaction between you and your message and the audience.

- Experts are often not the best communicators on their subject;

- The context message will establish a frame of reference in which you can operate – it is the 'big picture' or unmet need message;

- The news-hook – is the launch or announcement message – stating why the current event is important or significant;

- The call-to-action message sets out where next – what are the implications of the news-hook going forward – particularly for pre-identified stakeholders.

- There are two types of example: data – the more rational example – and hearts and minds – the more emotional example.

FIVE

On the Campaign Trail

Some messages are one offs, one time only exercises, constructed to serve a particular purpose. More common, however, is the situation where messages form part of a broader campaign. If you ask someone to marry you and they say "yes", that's a one time only message (hopefully). If you are less sure that your intended spouse will say yes, you may need to mount a more concerted campaign to persuade them of the obvious merits of such a union.

But what exactly is a campaign? Why is it important? And how does it work, both at an organisational and personal level? As a basic definition, a campaign is a sustained series of interventions around a single proposition, and that proposition must have some kind of emotional connect. A campaign involves a number of important elements.

Cultivating the grassroots

In order to create a campaign you must enlist numbers of people, both at the key opinion leader level, right down to the grassroots level.

THE MESSAGE

A key opinion leader is someone whose opinions on a particular subject command respect even if they are not academically or functionally associated with that particular subject.

So, for example, Bob Geldof would be a key opinion leader on the issue of developing nations, starvation and famine relief. Now Geldof's core competence was originally in the music business as a singer in the 1970s and 80s, for Irish new wave band The Boomtown Rats, where Geldof was more concerned about disliking Mondays than feeding the world.

But Geldof has since become, via Band Aid, a key opinion leader whose opinions are solicited by national leaders on the issue of developing nations. The value of enlisting key opinion formers, like Geldof, is that people respect them and their opinions and when they say something is so, then people tend to believe it.

So, for example, what if a key opinion leader like Geldof issued a statement that former President Bush had been a great force for good in Africa, in terms of the amount of aid work that Bush had backed. Now, supporting aid to Africa is not something that Bush is strongly associated with, but that sentiment would probably change, with more people inclined to associate Bush with the fight against famine in Africa, merely because Geldof has said that he is.

Or, if you want to take the issue of the environment, then you have people like Al Gore, former US presidential candidate, John Elkington, co-founder of SustainAbility and author of *Cannibals with Forks: The Triple Bottom Line of 21st Century Business*, and Jonathon Porritt, co-founder of Forum for the Future and former director of Friends of the Earth. All key opinion formers.

And just to reinforce the extent of the power that key opinion formers possess, a person like Bob Geldof would have more credibility on issues like world poverty and famine than many elected officials, indeed possibly more so than some national leaders.

And then, at the other end of the spectrum, there are the people popularly known as the grassroots. These are the activists, the people out on the streets, the people who knock on doors, corner people on the pavements, who wear the badges and the t-shirts. These are the people who are very enthused and evangelical about the issues. They might be the local members of Greenpeace, who are prepared to go out and tackle people over their stance on rain forests, and sustainable use of natural resources. Or they might be from Shelter, committed to housing the homeless.

So there are the professional activists, the people that go out and campaign on the street, and then there are the key opinion formers, the people who are able to impact public opinion and public policy at the same time. To mount an effective campaign you need to enlist a series of stakeholders all the way along the spectrum, as well as at the two extremes.

Hopes and fears

A campaign rarely evolves around an arid or rational idea, but usually around an emotional idea. The emotional tends to be more effective. In just the same way that it is important that a message has stickiness, so it applies to the wider campaign too. People tend to get involved when they feel emotionally compelled to do something.

THE MESSAGE

So campaigns usually revolve around a very simple idea packaged as some kind of proposition. The difference between an idea and a proposition being that a proposition has some type of impact on the audience, some sense of trying to enlist the other party to get involved in specific action.

This is in contrast to the expression of a bare idea or fact, which, as we have seen, in the new connected world usually elicits the response "so what". And it is the "so what" question, an increasingly common response to poorly constructed messages, that needs to be avoided. So, a proposition is an idea, plus a prompt to get involved; very action oriented.

One emotional driver is inspiration and beliefs that moves us towards bringing about a situation that reflects our concept of an ideal state of affairs. But another strong emotional driver is fear – fear that something we dread might happen, unless we get involved and prevent it from happening.

Time bound

As well as being driven by the emotions of inspiration, belief and fear, there is often a time element attached to a campaign. The time component is to heighten the sense for a need for action. So there may be a feeling that a certain event, or events, must occur by a certain time; the need to capture the moment, otherwise the opportunity to achieve the campaign's purpose will be missed. Alternatively, there may be a sense of needing to act before it is too late; before something terrible happens.

For example, London needs a better transport system, because it would improve the quality of everyone's lives who travel in the capital, allow people to be more productive, and hopefully improve pollution. The sooner this happens the less people will suffer from ill health due to increased pollution from the traffic jams; and the quicker the people in the capital will be able to improve productivity which will benefit the UK.

Or, we need to combat global warming and reduce carbon emissions to save the planet. We need to do this quickly, because if the level of carbon in the atmosphere rises above a certain point, then global warming may become irreversible, meaning the end of society as we know it.

Voluntary vs paid

As we have seen, for a campaign to be effective it needs to recruit people to its cause; both key opinion formers and grassroots activists. Success, however, should not be measured by the numbers of people recruited, but also by the types of people. And, in particular whether people recruited via the campaign are paid to bring about the campaign's desired aims, or volunteers.

Demonstrating that you have recruited volunteers to a cause, and having those volunteers evangelise your messages, and thereby your top line strategic aims, is usually more powerful, than having people evangelise you aims who are paid to do so. So when someone like Geldof steps up to talk about an issue, and they are not being paid to do that, you are more likely to believe that they are genuine in their passion for the cause. Whereas a paid spokesman for an organisation like an NGO carries less weight.

Message memo: Perception

Perception plays a very important, and often unperceived, role in messaging. If we talk at about 120 to 150 words per minute, we actually think at a rate of about 600 to 800, which means that when you are listening to a presentation unless you are completely engaged you mind will race ahead thinking about other things – like where you are going out that evening, or what else needs to go on the shopping list.

So this is a point where a disconnection can occur between the message and its recipient – as a listener returns to the message, after mentally completing their shopping list, only to realise they have missed a chunk.

The way that skilful communicators address the perception issue is instructive. Senator John McCain, during the recent Republican nominations, realised fairly early on that age was going to be a factor, as a lot of people commented on his age. The comments were indirectly questioning his capacity to do perform the demanding job of US President. And age was self-evidently not an issue for the youthful looking Barack Obama.

So what did McCain's team do to combat the negative comments about age?

Well the usual response in a situation like this, because it isn't the first time that this type of problem has emerged during apolitical campaign, is to send out the message that the politician in question has excellent stamina and physical health by showing clips of them jogging, walking up steep hills, exercising in various ways, briefing on their fitness regime etc.

> This time though the people in McCain's team appeared to come up with an alternative strategy. When McCain appeared for press conferences and other speechmaking opportunities he always seemed to be surrounded by a group of older people, with McCain looking youthful by comparison.
>
> As for Obama, his appearance also appeared tightly managed, limiting opportunities for any perception problems. Rarely, if ever, did you see Obama out of his "uniform" of white shirt and suit, during his nomination campaign. It is reminiscent of Andrea Merkel's successful campaign for chancellor of Germany where it seemed that she wore the same blue suit from the same designer throughout the whole election. Although, the blue suit was put back in the wardrobe once she was in power.
>
> Contrast this approach from that of Hillary Clinton during the Democratic nomination elections where there was huge variability in her appearance.

Personal campaigning

The word "campaign" may bring to mind NGOs like Greenpeace or Oxfam, or large corporations, however, it is possible to create a personal campaign as well, and quite easily, by using the same principles.

Individuals within organisations can also use a series of messages to construct a campaign, using emotional triggers to enlist key opinion formers and grassroots activists. There needs to be a reason for other people to act, otherwise the individual risks being seen as self-regarding or self-promoting, and consequently will not be able to engage with people as a result.

So, for example, an individual may be determined to obtain a promotion. In order to do so, they will have a target audience, for their messages and campaign. This may be their boss, but may also include their peers.

Personal campaigning is a situation where enlisting the help of fellow employees is also valuable. Achieving the strategic aim of promotion, might involve a number of different tactics. It might, for example, mean boosting personal sales figures, and exceeding sales targets. And, while members of the individual's organisation will all be being paid to do their individual jobs, the end target of which is to create shareholder value, they will not be being paid to assist your promotion.

The challenge then, is to use the messages to help recruit your team members and others, inside and outside the organisation, where appropriate, to meet your strategic campaign aim of achieving promotion, and at the same time meet aims which they ascribe value to. Finding alignment is not easy, but it can be done, and provides a very satisfying win-win situation.

Corporations vs NGOs

In the campaign stakes, corporations and the executives who orchestrate campaigns, tend not to be as sophisticated or as effective in their approach as NGOs. Look closely at the non government organisation versus the corporate organisation, and the structural advantages of the NGO soon become apparent. If campaigning was an ocean, NGOs would be the sharks, designed by evolution to hunt and eat, with every part of their anatomy geared up to facilitate that. Corporations by contrast are more whale like, often much larger than NGOs, but less efficient in terms of finding and consuming food.

Also NGOs usually have less at stake. If an NGO loses or fails in a campaign, then while the repercussions may be disastrous for the beneficiaries of the campaign, which by the way is usually not the NGO, the NGO will move on to another campaign, hopefully suffering little if any damage from the campaign failure.

If a corporation runs a campaign that fails, the fallout could be very damaging for a wide group of stakeholders associated with the company. There could be a significant adverse effect on shareholder value, on employee morale, even on levels of staffing, on relationships with customers, suppliers, and other stakeholders like local communities and government policymakers.

And, if you are the executive in charge of the campaign, then the personal stakes may also be quite high. You may lose your job.

BP is one example of a company that ran into some problems as result of a campaign failing to have the desired impact. In 2000 the company changed its name from British Petroleum to BP, and began a campaign entitled "Beyond Petroleum", it also adopted visual cues to support its new campaign including a new logo.

Unfortunately, a number of incidents related to BP's activities led to the company attracting some criticism from environmentalists who accused the company of greenwashing —proclaiming green credentials while polluting at the same time. These incidents included an explosion at BP's Texas City Refinery in Texas City, Texas in 2005, and an oil spill on the Alaskan tundra in 2006.

In touch with your emotions

One reason that many organisations find it difficult to run effective campaigns is that they are not willing to get emotional with the issues. Corporations and professional organisations tend to be quite controlled and not particularly fond of risk taking – even if they claim that they are.

So most organisations are fairly reserved when it comes to getting the Wow factor, creating an impact and setting out their stance in a way that grabs attention, and inspires or scares, or both in equal measures.

So an organisation like a leading FTSE 100 or Fortune 500 company, is unlikely to engage in the same kind of manoeuvres and stunts to create media attention, to create a spotlight on something, as am NGO such as Greenpeace might.

Major corporations do not really see it as their role to be attracting attention in the same way, they will release research papers and reports, make pronouncements, issue press releases, and orchestrate any campaign in a much more thorough, linear and usually quite rational way.

NGOs go for the jugular much more often, and that usually makes campaigning a lot easier because you go straight for the emotions, you show a picture of a baby seal getting battered across the white snow, or a group of children working in sweatshop. You can use an image like that get the headlines in the media, and then follow up with a very simple call to action and proposition, which is "we need to stop this now" – whether it is cruelty to seals, or child labour.

So NGOs are good at campaigns, and they have more freedom to create effective campaigns. When it comes to campaigning the NGOs and social movements are the place to go to for best practice, adopt their methods and principles, whether you are constructing a corporate or personal campaign, and you should not go too far wrong.

Serving two causes

We have already seen how it is possible to create a personal campaign that serves two causes, your own personal cause as well as that of the organisation that you work for.

In the same way companies can create campaigns that serve two causes, a corporate cause, directed at creating shareholder value, as well as some kind of societal cause. And this dual cause campaign can prove highly effective, enlisting people to the societal cause, while also recruiting them as consumers.

A good example is Unilever and its Dove soap campaigns. By using "real" women in its advertisements, Unilever made a statement against the use of conventional advertising stereotypes of beautiful "perfect" women in advertising. And by engaging in a very powerful debate around the fact that women are being overly pressurised by unreal images of beauty the Dove soap brand was able to position itself as a much more consumer friendly proposition. In this way Unilever managed to campaign for two causes at the same time – one corporate, one social.

Unilever also reached out with its messages and campaign through a variety of mediums, including, for example, YouTube where there are a number of clips highlighting the artificiality of beauty as used in advertising, by revealing the way a make up team and retouching of photos by computer programme are used to create the final image. One clip – Evolution – for example, has a less glamorous looking lady getting made up, and then she is transformed into a stunning beauty by the end of it, revealing the illusory nature of beauty in advertising.

So there is a corporate campaign making a contribution to a social debate, which has been really welcomed by their core audience, who are celebrating the fact that a company has the courage to put ordinary non-model women on billboards.

In fact Unilever has a history of environmental campaigning, in 1997, the company, which buys a lot of fish for production purposes, set up the Marine Stewardship Council (MSC) in association with the World Wide Fund for Nature (WWF). The objective of the organisation and its campaigns is to promote sustainable fisheries and responsible fishing practices. The founding of the council, and the subsequent campaign, has helped the world's fish stocks, but it has also helped boost Unilever's credibility on corporate social responsibility issues.

Call to action

So where do messages fit within the campaign? Call to action messages are future oriented, emotionally driven, trying to enlist the act of support, and engagement of the audience, with a cause in mind. So it is really the call to action messages that we are discussing with respect to campaigns.

Examples of campaigns

Political – Obama vs Clinton

Politicians are well versed in the art of the campaign, and usually campaign on a combination of belief, with a little bit of fear mixed in. So, "believe in me, I can do this for our economy", or on the fear side, "if you don't vote for me then things won't go as well as you might think".

Hillary Clinton used the fear factor, to some degree, in her campaign for the Democratic presidential nomination. One of the tactics of the campaign was to use messages to question Barack Obama's ability to manage a foreign affairs crisis. So the fear component was evident in terms of being unable to trust Obama to do a good job as President because of his lack of experience.

However, despite all the negative campaigning and scare tactics that often surface during political campaigning, politicians, for the most part are belief based operators. They try to inspire people with a vision of the future, and then go through the process of enlisting people with a campaign that will encompass a range of message delivery methods, from television advertising, debates and rallies, to pressing the flesh, getting out on the stump and meeting people to deliver a personal verbal message, kissing babies, and beginning to engender a glow and coalesce support around a particular idea for which they are the change agent.

NGO – Genetic modification

NGOs often like to appear, and do appear, to be amateurish, in the sense that they appear "real", they grow in an organic and

THE MESSAGE

sometimes haphazard way, and are full of enthusiasm. This is because a campaign that appears too slick and overly professional may be equated with artifice, simulation and concealment. Do not be fooled, though, NGOs campaign in a highly professional manner, and while there will be many amateur activists involved in an NGO's campaign, the campaign itself will usually be orchestrated be experienced professionals.

The NGOs operate primarily via fear. The offer a vision of the future whereby if certain action is not taken then the existing state of affairs will continue, which is unacceptable, or will get worse, and this will have a seriously adverse affect for something or someone. And the closer the campaign and messaging can bring those adverse effects to the person receiving the message, the better.

So, for example, if the issue is nuclear technology and the NGO is anti nuclear power then the message is going to be that you may end up with a nuclear power station in your backyard, that nuclear waste is going to get into the food chain, that power is going to have a harmful impact on the health of your children. This, despite the fact that nuclear power might actually be necessary in a world of declining fuel resources.

So the NGOs and similar organisations will also paint a picture of a rosier future, but ultimately they operate much more on the fear basis that x has to stop, you can help it stop, and if you don't, it will a) continue or b) get worse; so get involved.

Also, NGOs, like WWF, Greenpeace, and Friends of the Earth are populated by professional activists, and while they may run specific individual campaigns they are in it for the long run. When one campaign is finished they will move onto the next.

ON THE CAMPAIGN TRAIL

Personal Campaigns: Find Madeline, Surfers against Sewage

Personal campaigns are, by their very nature, much more fragmented. They may adopt either the belief or fear approach. Find Madeline, for example, was a combination of both. Partly it was about making society a better place for families. So, we will all need to help find this girl because society shouldn't be like this. Families should be able to go on holiday and not have to worry about the safety of their children.

But there was also the element of fear. Particularly for parents of children that looked like Madeline, or were the same age, there was an element of this could happen to your child, how would you cope if it did?

Also personal campaigns tend to end when the result is achieved, or the campaign fails. When a group of local villagers get together to campaign against the erection of mobile phone masts, for example, or a wind farm, the campaign usually finishes when planning permission is either granted or refuse, (after appeals), or it may lie dormant until the matter is revived. If you are mounting a personal campaign to get promoted, your campaign will end when you make promotion, or at such times as you realise you are not going to get promoted.

Alternatively, some campaigns start out on a personal level and then broaden out to become more NGO like, addressing a wider spectrum of issues.

Surfers Against Sewage (SAS) was founded in 1990 by a group of surfers in Cornwall, who decided to campaign because they were constantly getting ill as a result of the pollution of sea water by sewage. The campaign might easily have stayed personal and its activities restricted to improving the water quality in surfing location in Cornwall. No doubt when water quality improved sufficiently the campaign would have stopped.

However, SAS struck a chord with other recreational water users, and instead of winding down it has expanded its remit to include "a broader range of water issues that can impact both on the health of the water user and that of the water environment". So campaigns include Sewage and Sickness', 'Safer Shipping', 'No To Toxics', and 'Climate Chaos'.

Remember too, that sincerity is essential with personal campaigns. In a personal campaign the messages are connected directly to you and your reputation. If you are found out to be deceiving or manipulating, lying, or being economical with the truth, then your own credibility will be tainted, and the damage to your reputation may be irreparable.

As we have seen, individuals within organisations can also run personal campaigns. So that might be on a matter of organisational values, whether it is improving communications with consumers, looking after younger employees better, or restructuring the organisation in a much more sympathetic way than it is doing. Equally, a campaign could be about personal visibility, getting a promotion more quickly, or allowing an employees' vision of the future of the business to be enacted.

GET THE MESSAGE

- An effective use of messages is to include them in a broader campaign.

ON THE CAMPAIGN TRAIL

- A campaign is a sustained series of interventions around a single proposition, and that proposition must have some kind of emotional connect.

- In a campaign you need to cultivate the grassroots activists, as well as the opinion leaders.

- Campaign messaging is often driven by focusing on either hopes or fears.

- Discrete campaigns tend to have some time limit attached.

- Campaigns work both on an organisational and individual level; with personal campaign you need to align organisational and personal goals.

SIX

Welcome to the Grid
Managing the Messages

As well as understanding the components of a message and how to create messages, organisations and individuals need to understand the tactics and strategies for using messages. We have already looked at the Context, News Hook and Call to Action, aspects of the Message Grid (see Figure 2) and The message grid allows us to transpose these across three different areas; product and service, market and thought leadership.

Ultimately, the value of the Grid for an organisation or individual is that it is a tool that can be used to ensure that you speak with one voice across the organisation. It allows different people within an organisation to speak to other people with different agendas, on different timelines, short, medium or long term, and yet still appear in harmony. So it, it is a harmonising device.

It is organised along three tranches of leadership, the assumption being that the speaker or the organisation, the message sender, wants to establish some type of primacy, hence the word, leadership. And in doing so, is able to recruit people, we can call them stakeholders, to the cause that they are trying to promote.

THE MESSAGE

Message Grid

	PRODUCT LEADERSHIP Innovation today - solution of choice (targets users)	MARKET LEADERSHIP Where the sector is going Targets partners customers eg purchasers, supply chain, employees, financial community	THOUGHT LEADERSHIP How the sector is going to get there (Targets Government, regulators, NGOs)
Context Message (Aerial perspective - establishes authority)			
EXAMPLES			
News-Hook Message (Reason for communicating right now - establishes topicality)			
EXAMPLES			
Call-to-action Message (Looks to the future - prompts action)			
EXAMPLES			

Figure 2

Product leadership

Product leadership, as the name suggests, concerns the service or the product being sold. It would usually focus on some difference, some innovation, that distinguishes the message sender's products and services from others.

So if we take an example of product leadership and apply it to the Grid it might look something like this.

Let's take Diageo and the beer business in Japan in 2006. Diageo was dealing with a situation where there was not enough room in pubs

WELCOME TO THE GRID: MANAGING THE MESSAGES

in Japan to store kegs of Guinness stout properly. The bars were small, and often there was no cellar room, as with conventional pubs in the Ireland and the UK, for example.

The Japanese still wanted to present pints of Guinness in the best possible way. It was a problem that many vendors of Guinness faced where they did not have the space or the turnover to offer draught Guinness.

So, after some research and development, the people at Diageo came up with a novel solution. The pints of Guinness would be poured at the counter, and then they would be sat on a "Surger" unit, which pulsed sound waves through the pint, conjuring up the famous Guinness head associated with draught Guinness.

The context message in this situation would be, that if storage space is at a premium or turnover is low, or there are other reasons that you cannot store and offer draught Guinness, then there is still a solution that will allow you to satisfy consumer demand for a beer that looks like the traditional Guinness pint. So you do not need to keep beer in a cellar to sell a pint of Guinness.

The news hook is that Diageo are allowing people to create the traditional Guinness head on a pint poured from a can, using new sound wave technology, with their Surger unit. And it was a news hook that worked well because the new technology was covered extensively in the press.

And, finally, the call to action message is for customers to come and try the Guinness presented in this way.

It is worth noting that, all the other components of the message need to be in place, and that includes the piece about a message not being wallpaper that papers over problems with a product or service. The product, in this case Guinness, still has to taste good to consumers, it still has to be of sufficient quality, and no amount of zapping with sound waves is going to change that.

So it was interesting to see that when Guinness brewmaster Fergal Murray, showcased the new gadget in Australia, he was tackled by at least one journalist on whether there had been a decline in quality of the product, as some commentators were saying.[1] It is a reminder that you need to get the basics right with your product, service or whatever the subject of your message is, as well as getting the messaging right.

Market leadership

The thing with product leadership is that it is all about the now. It is short term, revolving around current innovations, and what is happening today. It is also focused on specific products and services – so Guinness beer, for example and aimed primarily at the consumer. The organisation wants the consumer to know about the special attributes or innovations associated with its product or service.

Market leadership targets different types of people, it has a different subject as its focus, and is looking at different timescales. So market leadership revolves around indicating where the sector or the category is going. Is a particular sector or category going up or going down; shrinking or increasing. Is a company on the move or is it facing difficulties.

---

[1] www.news.com.au/couriermail/story/0,23739,20549937-5004581,00.html

WELCOME TO THE GRID: MANAGING THE MESSAGES

In terms of time market leadership is about the medium to long term, not the here and now. It looks at trends and direction over a longer time horizon.

It could be processed foods, for example, that is a category, and the trend in the sector is that people are much more inclined to want ready made meals for microwaves, than to prepare a fresh meal. That trend is down to a lot of different factors, demographics, living styles, work pressures, and many others.

The audience for the market leadership message includes people like employees, the financial community, and investors. So what is happening to the category or sector over the next six months, or year, or eighteen months.

A context message might be, for example, that a particular market is facing a price squeeze through consolidation. Consolidation in the market is making things more competitive and therefore the organisation is going to restructure to cut costs and get closer to the customer. The news hook would be what the message sender intends to do or launch as a response to this trend

A Call to Action message would set out what the receiver needs to do with regard to this initiative, what they might, for example, implement or how they might adapt, as a result. It might be that the organisation needs to become more flexible; to structure working practices in way that allows the organisation to be more adaptable.

Thought leadership

Thought leadership is about shaping messages; messages that

actually describe the environment itself with a view to establishing a playing field that is going to allow your organisation to be more successful.

The audiences here are non-governmental organisations, governments, policymakers, opinion formers and shapers. There is a popular saying "the world is run by those people who show up," and it is very true. If you participate in long term debates, you shape the way that society flows. If you are at the negotiations table, you help shape the outcome of those negotiations. You have to engage to influence.

So many people complain about the politicians that represent them, but you get the politicians you deserve—because those are the people that are prepared to get involved. In the same way it is pointless complaining about the competence of the project leader that volunteered for the job, if you were not prepared to volunteer.

Organisations can shape the future, but only if they take a position and then engage on the wider debate on the issues that concern them. The timeframe here is long term; you will be looking at three to five years.

If we take technology, for example, Microsoft versus its competitors might be an example of thought leadership.

The context message here would be that the technology landscape is being dominated by too few players. The news hook would be that the attempts by Microsoft to buy Yahoo show that there is a situation which may potentially lead to less rather than more consumer choice. The call to action is that we need to legislate to ensure that consumer choice does not suffer as a result of these large seismic shifts in the technology world.

Another technology debate that organisations need to embrace at the moment, particularly Internet technology companies, is net neutrality. The idea the Internet should be open to all rather than a walled garden where ISPs control and restrict access.

In the case of net neutrality, the context message might be about the need for unfettered access to the Internet and the possibility that broadband carriers might restrict that access. The news hook is that certain organisations are considering prioritising access to Internet content, depending on how much content providers will pay. The call to action is that net neutrality cannot be left to the market but needs to be protected by enacting legislation.

Credibility counts

The reason that this grid is important is that because it delivers a harmonious perspective to the market. Why is harmony important, or better than disharmony in a web 2.0 world and a post-modern existence? Why is harmony better than pluralistic dialogue? Because the need here is to deliver consistency. The reason that consistency is important is that consistency is very closely allied to credibility.

Credibility is the currency of communication. There is no point in having the right words if your credibility is low, the people who do not believe, will not buy into your message anyway. And the reason why consistency impacts credibility is that, very quickly, if you say one thing today and say something different tomorrow, people then start distrusting your motives. So using the Grid enables you to consistent and therefore credible.

Equally, if you say something today and then you behave differently, then again, people see a difference between what you say and what you do. Credibility goes down as a result and your ability communicate effectively suffers. So, it is very important to try and maintain a consistent perspective on things, or at least have an explanation for any lack of consistency.

So, for example, if an organisation says that it is very people-focused, one big, happy family, but then behaves poorly through a restructuring process, you have got inconsistency between message and behaviour. Then people will begin to doubt the company pronouncements not only on the family oriented nature of the business, but also on other matters as well. So it is very important for an organisation to try and manage credibility as clearly as possible.

Quite often that credibility is managed through the persona of the Chief Executive himself. If the CEO or another senior executive has a high profile then that individual's persona will be part of the credibility equation, in addition to specific transactions that are happening.

However, in the majority of organisations, and certainly those with a lot of personnel change, it will be the corporate brand, rather than any particular individual, that carries responsibility for maintaining credibility, and therefore the organisation will need to try and manage its communications sometimes through very rapidly moving events on a global scale, in a consistent fashion. It is a very hard task to accomplish, but demonstrating the will to be consistent, has in itself a rigour and discipline that people will appreciate.

WELCOME TO THE GRID: MANAGING THE MESSAGES

Managing the unmanageable

Managing the message is a complex organisational challenge. The Message Grid, therefore, is an extremely useful tool, providing a framework for consistency, keeping control of and monitoring the organisational wide approach to messages.

In the 21st century, however the message management challenge has taken a turn for the impossibly complicated. Organisational messages used to be comparatively easy to manage, once the organisation had committed to managing them because they were produced by the organisation in a controlled process.

Today, however, technology has liberated employees to communicate with the external world in ways that were not possible before. The blog is a prime example of this. Many employees are blogging about what goes on in the workplace. In some cases, when the CEO or other executives are doing the blogging, or even further down the hierarchy, the blogging is part of the managed message process. Other employees, however, are blogging without the permission of their employer. This means unmanaged communication; with unpredictable results.

No longer are words just funnelled through a couple of public relations or media spokespeople, or given the once over by the legal team. Instead a fairly unmanaged, sometimes irreverent stream of communication is emanating, virtually, from organisations, and is then picked up on by the media, as a well as a range of stakeholders. In this situation consistency becomes almost impossible.

THE MESSAGE

Using the Grid for your own ends

Although the Grid is a tool that is primarily used to maintain harmony and consistency of messages across a number of different people, with minor modifications, it can also be a very useful tool for a single individual, or an individual who is communicating with a personal, rather than organisational agenda.

Just as organisations need to manage, control and coordinate messages emanating from sometimes thousands of employees around the globe, using a variety of mediums, individuals also have to manage their messages, even if not on such a substantial scale.

So, for example, career progression is partly about personal brand. That is, if you adopted a brand perspective, to managing your career, you would establish your brand values, and positioning, you would have certain things about you which you want other people to understand, and then you would need to represent your personal brand in a consistent and controlled way.

All the time, you are sending out messages about yourself which affect the way that other people perceive you, both in work, and generally as a person. Those messages will relate to the present, the here and now, to the near future, six months to a year down the road, as well as to the more distant future. And, regardless of whether your messages relate to today, or five years in the future, you need to be consistent and to manage perceptions.

Consequently, an individual could look at the Grid in terms of short, medium or long term planning, and delivering their messages to a number of different stakeholders.

WELCOME TO THE GRID: MANAGING THE MESSAGES

Message memo: What the dooce?

Blogging is mainstream. Even senior executives are getting in on the act. Now anyone and everyone can discover the innermost thoughts, hopes and fears of the great and good of business, or some of them at least.

At the last count, a quick Google search revealed that General Motors –yes that traditional non hi-tech auto industry company –has a blog, posted up by tech savvy septuagenarian vice chairman Bob Lutz. Joseph B. Wikert, a vice president at publishing outfit Wiley, has Joe Wikert's Publishing 2020 Blog. Not to forget the inside-the-company view from Sun Microsystems president and COO, Jonathan Schwartz.

A note of caution though, for those who are about to join, or already are, part of the blogging community. According to a Workplace E-Mail, Instant Messaging & Blog Survey from American Management Association (AMA) and The ePolicy Institute, nearly 2% of companies surveyed had fired workers -that's dooced in blogger language -for posting offensive blog content—including posts on employees' personal home-based blogs.

Only 9 % of organisations had policies in place to cover business blogging; and only 7 % had rules governing the content posted by employees on their home based personal blogs.

A famous victim of blogging fallout is Ellen Simonetti, a former flight attendant in the US who worked for Delta Airlines. Simonetti posted pictures of herself in her work uniform on her blog Queen of Sky: Diary of a Dysfunctional Flight Attendant. The snaps were deemed inappropriate by her employers. You can check out the pics on her retitled blog – Queen of Sky: Diary of a Fired Flight Attendant.

Equally, for those running internal campaigns which are primarily serving personal aims, although they may be serving organisational objectives as a by-product, and are personally driven, the Grid can still be a very useful tool. This is because a personal campaign will be designed to recruit various other people to your cause, and may well co-opt others into delivering your messages, therefore planning for consistency across types of messages and timescales is just as important for you, as it is for an organisation.

GET THE MESSAGE

- The Message Grid is a harmonising device that allows you to manage your messages more effectively, ensuring that you are consistent in your approach, across timescales and agendas.

- The Grid is organised across three facets of leadership: product leadership; market leadership, and thought leadership.

- The Grid is also a useful tool for managing messages that relate to your own personal brand.

SEVEN

The Go-Between

Filtering

The consumer, whether it is a private individual or a business, receives hundreds if not thousands of messages every week. And as most employees already know, they too are swamped with a deluge of messages courtesy of both internal communications and as part of the need to keep up with consumer oriented messages.

Just look at the messages that people are bombarded with from the tech sector alone. With 11,000 plus major companies in the tech sector, and hundreds of thousands of smaller companies worldwide all plying their trade, that adds up to some tens of thousands of news releases every day, and many tens of thousands of messages delivered via the full panoply of media. A quick perusal of the Microsoft website, for example, reveals anything from one to ten plus press releases a day.

While some of the messages go directly from the creator of the message to the recipient, many do not. To get from creator to

THE MESSAGE

recipient, messages need to be delivered. Delivery can take place via a huge range of media, from the telephone to the Internet, from business cards to junk mail. Many messages, conference talks, team meeting presentations, best man's speeches, will be delivered directly to the recipient, without a third party getting in the way between the creation of the message and its audience. Assuming that the messages just mentioned are delivered by the people that wrote them, of course.

Often, however, messages will be delivered by third parties and go-betweens. As these messages flow towards the consumer they roll through a set of influences. They get filtered, and then filtered again, before finally reaching an audience.

In computing and linguistics the terms encoding and decoding are used to describe the packing and unpacking of information. In the flow of business and organisational information, information passes along the chain of intermediaries with each decoding then recoding the information in a corporate version of Chinese whispers (or Telephone, as it is known in the US) [see Box]. The more intermediaries they pass through, the more messages are at risk of becoming distorted. This is often forgotten when producing messages.

Messages are written with the end audience in mind, it might be the consumer, or if it is internal communications, for the employee. Yet, when you are constructing a message, you must also be writing for the recoders; for the group of people that deliver the message to the consumer on the organisation's behalf. These people are often other employees of the organisation – especially the employees in sales and marketing, dealing directly with consumers. Or you might be writing for a message ambassador; a disciple of the organisation prepared to evangelise the message.

THE GO-BETWEEN

> **Message memo: The broken telephone**
>
> The childhood game, known as Chinese whispers in the UK, or the many other names it goes by around the world – The broken telephone, Operator, Grapevine, Whisper Down the Lane – dates back to at least the 17th century in the UK, and probably beyond. It is a wonderful example of the burden of responsibility on intermediaries.
>
> Around the world, the game has different names. Telephone in the US, Ticha Posta or Silent Mail in the Czech Republic and Slovakia, 'pass wrong with wrong' in Mandarin, (or so Wikipedia tells us).
>
> The world record for the biggest whispering chain is 614 people. The event took place in Las Vegas in 2004, when Mac King a magician, started the whisper off with 'Mac King is a comedy magic genius'. By the time it reached the end of the line the message had become 'Macaroni cantaloupe knows the future'.

Targeting the intermediary

Perhaps the most obvious and influential group of people in an organisation to get involved in message delivery is the sales force. Indeed in many businesses the sales force is probably the most important recoder of communication.

The media is a good example of the power of the recoder. Many newspapers, for example, have a tendency to reflect the beliefs and opinions of their proprietors. The papers take the raw material of news, either from the news agencies, or directly from reporters on the ground, and report it with more or less spin added by the newspaper itself. Dealt with in this way news becomes a product.

TV production companies are the same, using editing to shape content. A common complaint of the subjects of reality programming or fly on the wall documentaries is that the programme was cut in a way that portrayed them in certain light.

In most organisations, the communications team is geared up to focus its attention on the final recipient of the message –the consumer, or employee. However, it is also essential to take into account how an intermediary may interpret and translate a message, whether it is the media, or as is commonly the case the sales force.

So one of the challenges that companies have to solve is how to identify and deal with the recoders, and while that may involve a wide range of people from within the organisation, and outside it,

Selling the right message

A key element of many message processes, is where the salesperson acts as an interface between corporate messaging and customer, whether B-to-B or B-to-C. And remember that through our interactions with other people, whether customers, the general public, or other employees, we are all salespeople for the organisations we work for.

One CIO of a major corporation once gave us some very useful advice. The senior executive, who controlled multi billion dollars worth of spend, was giving a presentation to some marketing

THE GO-BETWEEN

people. Yes, he explained, he did receive the presentational material that the marketing executives sent him. He also looked at the company's press releases every now and then, as well as checking on the media coverage to check if it was positive or bad.

But, he said, at the end of the day, he got the information he really needed from the salesperson. If he did not trust the salesperson, then he would not buy from them. If he did not like the salesperson, he would not buy from them. If he did not feel that the salesperson cared, and was informed and knowledgeable, he would not buy from them. Not much else mattered. It was all about the way the salesperson delivered the company's message.

And we heard similar tales from many other senior executives with significant buying power. Unless you get it right for the salesperson, you will lose out. It is difficult to understand the damage that an intermediary can do to an excellently fashioned message until you witness it at first hand, as a friend of ours did.

Indeed a great example of how the salesperson can intervene in an unintended way happened when someone we knew decided that it was time to replace their Lexus motor car with an Acura MDX, the luxury Honda marque.

Getting a replacement car had been on the cards for some time. Over a period of several months we had, at various times, politely teased the person that the Acura was just an expensive Honda. Our friend's stock response to this comment was that was like saying a Lexus is a Toyota, so why not buy a Toyota. The MDX was, our friend argued, not "just an expensive Honda", but totally different.

Finally, one weekend, our friend took a trip to the local car dealership. First impressions were not good; the place appeared a bit disorganised. But then the salesman came over. He was smiling, looked reasonably smart, and was hopefully about to dispel any negative impressions.

Our friend explained, at some length, exactly what they were looking for, how very impressed they were with the Acura range, that they had wanted to buy one for some time and had finally decided now was the moment. At which point the salesman told our friend that he had just come over from the Honda dealership, and although he did not know so much about Acuras, he could talk about Hondas all day long.

That was an example of an employee assigned to deliver a message, and getting it wrong. It was a message at odds with the brand. If the salesman had asked us for our advice, for example, at least with a view to selling to our friend, we would have told him on no account to mention the word Honda.

Our friend wanted to buy a luxury car to replace his existing luxury car. What is the point of spending a lot of money developing a luxury car brand, and the appropriate luxurious car messaging to accompany it, if you then remind prospective purchasers of its possibly less luxurious antecedents? After all a quick visit to the Acura website, and the About Acura section and you are hard pushed to find a mention of "Honda."

Why did this happen? Perhaps because the salesman in this case had not been briefed about the brand message and how their actions impacted on that message. Without strong direction from an organisation it is very easy for their employees to lose their way when they are interpreting and reinterpreting organisational messages.

Maverick communicators

Organisations should not only worry about the accidental twisting or damaging of messages by their intermediaries, but also about the purposeful creation of messages intended for the consumer.

Interestingly, according to the American Marketing Association, sales representatives spend 35 per cent of their time creating messaging for prospects. So the communications people, or the ad agency, or the internal marketing team, spend 100 per cent of their time carefully crafting messages, and message campaigns, and the sales teams in their own wisdom decide to create their own messages.

This means that, at any given time, a multinational corporation probably has thousands of sales people out in the market, not delivering any of the messages that the communications people have spent a good amount of time and work creating. And instead, whether because they have decided they do not like the organisational messaging, or they are not aware of it, or they are not trained properly, they are out in the market each delivering their own messages – random messaging, something all organisations should work hard to avoid.

So despite what you may think, or hope, often what you think is being told to customers, is not being told to customers. In one organisation, for example, one executive developed an organisational presentation about the future of information technology. This presentation proved popular and so the sales reps in a business unit of the organisation in another territory asked to use the presentation, and then videoed it.

A while later the executive who created original asked to see the version of the presentation that was being used in this territory. When it arrived he was surprised to find that was completely different. As he described it looked "like it was created by kindergarten children, who had cut and pasted images into it."

And besides the way it looked, in terms of content it was also off message, being more about sustainability and green issues than the original concept of the future of IT. So at events in this particular territory where, as far as the senior communications team was aware, the corporation's message about the future of IT was being delivered, in reality the sales people were reinventing the message and delivering a message about green issues. And not necessarily the organisation's own stance on green issues, either.

This is not just a message issues, although that element is particularly important, it is also a productivity problem. The communications people are spending time figuring out what the right message is, how it should be articulated, how it can be localised, how it can be made relevant, and then the sales teams for an area on the other side of the world are spending a good proportion of their time doing the same thing with different results. So there is a huge amount of inefficiency in organisational messaging, and one of the most important audiences to get to, in the commercial sense, is actually not the customer but the salesperson, who is acting as corporate message intermediary.

Monitoring the messenger

One reason that the sales people, and others, are inventing their own messages, is because it is so easy to with the help of modern technology. Information is democratised. With consumers running riot creating blogs and reviews, it is easy for them to criticise products and services in a way that is easy for everyone to access. After all, consumers appear to be more motivated to express their opinions about a product or service when they find something wrong with it. Freely available consumer feedback, however, much of it negative, can lead to an uncoordinated reactive response from sales in terms of messaging.

The same democratisation of information can also lead to temptation for the sales force in terms of messaging. Google just about any "subject + ppt" and you will find examples of other organisations' presentations on that issue. From there is a small step to mash up other presentations and make your own. The surfeit of available information means that the sales people and others within the organisation feel sufficiently empowered and informed to create and develop their own messages.

Or you can go to Slide Share, where it seems an army of PowerPoint equipped executives have posted up their work for the world to share.

So if you are tasked with creating and monitoring messages within an organisation, you need to keep up to speed on the latest developments on the Internet for presentation creation, as well as other message creation tools, and then you need to track your message implementation and message adoption with the intermediaries.

And if you are an intermediary, tasked with delivering a message, remember to preserve the integrity of the original message in any reinterpretation or recoding that you do. It may be tempting to deliver your own message, or what you see as your own version of the original message, but in doing so you are undermining the organisation's overall communications strategy.

THE MESSAGE

Message memo: Finding the right words

Great messages are rooted in words. It may sounds obvious, but as we find ourselves repeating over and over, to become a good communicator it is vital that you read a lot. And once you become proficient at communicating, then you need to keep reading. It is important to keep pace with changes in the use of language.

New words are added to the dictionary every year. Recent additions to the Oxford Concise dictionary include twonk, celebutante and crunk.

And make sure that your reading covers a wide range of media, styles and forms. Read hard copy, like newspapers – the red tops and the old broadsheets, magazines, academic journals, trade press, packaging, books of a variety of genres, advertising copy, promotional materials, CD covers, and much more.

Look at the use of words online, in blogs, corporate profiles, executive bios, online journalism, product and service reviews, advertising, social networking interaction, messaging, twittering, and SMS.

Of particular interests are the transcripts of speeches, the famous, like Churchill and JFK and the less famous, like the many CEO speeches you can access via corporate websites.

This level of word consumption will acclimatise you to the different ways that words are used in various media, and the patterns of words that people and organisations use.

Because so often it is the poor use of words that sabotages our best efforts to communicate. It is lazy use of words, instead of really thinking about whether the words you have chosen are the right words for the audience. Or whether the message is framed in the right way.

There a many words that should be avoided, depending on the organisation or individual involved. For Microsoft, for example, it is probably a good idea to avoid the word "dominate" in messaging internal or external. After all, the abuse of a dominant position in a market is something that Microsoft has been repeatedly accused of.

And a global corporation might choose to avoid using the word "market" as it might make a multinational corporation appear more parochial than it would like. Multinational corporations operate in countries and economies after all.

CTC: Critical to customer

One reason that the sales force is so keen to change messages originating from the organisation's communications department is that often the messages produced do not support what the sales team is trying to achieve.

This highlights the need to understand what is CTC (critical to customer). What matters most to the customer? And that in turn means understanding elements of the business such as the sales cycle.

The sales cycle goes something like this: Generate a lead; convert the lead into a prospect or opportunity; put that in a pipeline, and manage the pipeline and sales opportunities; then convert to sales prospect to a revenue opportunity – close the deal and sell to the customer.

This is an ongoing process that is based on relationships and takes place over varying timescales often extending to months, and years. Yet messages tend to focus on the end point and the consumer. They ignore the lengthy relationship building and management process.

When the organisation has a new widget in the pipeline it usually is not reluctant to trumpet its forthcoming offering. The sales team, however, may be far from impressed by the new messages. For someone who has just spent the last six months persuading a customer of the merits of the old widget, the news that they will probably need to go through the same process all over again, is unlikely to be well received.

What the sales people really need are messages that support them at different phases of the sales cycle. So is it a message that helps to activate a sale? Or one that helps to enforce a sales opportunity? Or is the message providing supporting evidence for the sales cycle, helping to secure and close a sale.

A good example is where larger organisations, particularly in the technology sector, make a lot of acquisitions. Yet they fail to translate these acquisitions into messages that support sales. What should be happening is for the organisations to equip people with messages that explain how the services and products provided by the newly acquired companies enhance the relationship between the organisation and the consumer, or the existing products and services provided by the organisation.

And although the focus has been on people who work in sales of some sort, because they are the most common intermediary, as we made clear earlier most people act as an intermediary for delivering, messages at some point.

GET THE MESSAGE

- It would be impossible to deal with the amount of information, and messages, we come into contact with, without applying some sort of internal filtering.

- Most messages travel through one or more intermediaries before reaching their audience and this accentuates the filtering effect. As a result messages become distorted.

- Message creators need to take into account, and target message intermediaries to ensure that the integrity and meaning of the original message is maintained.

- One of the most common intermediaries is the sales person.

- Watch out for maverick communicators, intermediaries determined to pursue their own message agenda.

- If you are intermediary, take care to deliver the same message you were entrusted with.

EIGHT

You've Been Framed

A managed process

Messaging should be part of a managed process. It is the "managed" aspect that distinguishes messaging from simple sharing ideas or information. After all, we communicate all of the time with family, friends, and colleagues, we share ideas, insights and anecdotes. But most of the time we do this without an overarching agenda or a cause.

With organisational business communication, however, (and sometimes with personal communication), we are often serving various organisational agendas, and that is where messaging comes in; it is absolutely key to being able to drive and add value to that process.

Framing is one of the key tools for either the individual or the organisation to begin to shape the world of the audience that will be receiving the message and then hopefully taking some action as result. So framing is really a tactical weapon in a managed communication process.

Establishing primacy

All of the time as a goal of the managed communication process, you are trying to create a space, that is going to contribute to the organisation establishing leadership or primacy.

So you could see the frame as a corral, which marks out the boundaries of the territory that you are going to own. Delineating the boundaries, or the terms of reference, not only establishes the territory, it also serves as controlling measure for the audience. You are trying to get the audience into the corral, pen them in and keep them there.

The, context and the call-to action messages discussed earlier help to peg out the coordinates of the corral. You establish the big picture and then you try and tell the audience what they need to do.

Smoking in the frame

Think back to the 1950s and 60s when smoking was all the rage and the tobacco companies were able to deny and then confuse the link between human health and the activity of smoking; they were able to have a licence to operate and market their products freely.

When the US Surgeon General's report into the hazards of smoking was followed in 1966 by the now familiar warning on cigarette packets – in this case "Caution: Cigarette Smoking May be Hazardous to Your Health" – that set out the fact smoking is bad for your health, it started a new dynamic for the smoking industry where it really was just a matter of time before the game was up when it came to the issue of smoking and its negative effects on health.

What the tobacco companies then began to do, as a result of the attention given to the link between smoking and ill-health, was to reframe the debate towards the issue of consumer choice, which they have accomplished quite successfully. So the tobacco companies are no longer just purveyors of fine tobacco; they are now ambassadors for consumer choice and the rights of the individual smoker to exercise their choice to smoke.

This is very clever tactical move as part of a wider managed communication process as it began to shift the debate from whether smoking was good or bad for your health, because opinion is fairly clear cut on that issue, to whether the individual smoker has a right to choose to smoke.

So there is a classic example of an industry, and the companies within it, reshaping and reframing the issue around which they are messaging, and it has allowed the tobacco companies continued social licence to operate.

Framing is not spinning

Using framing in this way and establishing the field of play, the frame of reference, on which the organisation intends to provide information about a subject, a product or service, or debate an issue, is not about spin doctoring or making things sound better, but actually core to how organisations survive and prosper.

To find their frame organisations tend to go beyond the superficial digging down, for example, to their founding principles. They ask questions like what makes us successful, what underpins our drive forward in the marketplace.

Message memo: Rooted in values

Great messages stand for something. Great messages are always rooted in values. So when you are putting a message together you need to consider what values you are aligning it with. It is important to make sure the values are consistent with your objectives, organisational or personal.

Take the situation in the US where there are many people unable, for one reason or another, to have a bank account. This presents the problem for some people of how to cash their weekly pay cheque. So, for an organisation like Wal-Mart, the US discount store giant, the message that it allows its customers to cash pay cheques at customer service desks, fits perfectly with its values of customer value and service, and Everyday Low Prices. It is not, however, a message that most luxury high-end brands would want to endorse, given that exclusivity is part of their ethos.

Another good example of how messages and values can align is Revlon the US cosmetics company, which began selling its cosmetics in chemists as well as in department stores.

Telling consumers that the company's products were now available in chemists might seem like an appropriate message for a company which until that point only sold its cosmetics through department stores. But not when you learn of a remark by the company's founder Charles Revson, who said: "We don't sell cosmetics, we sell hope." It was the kind of hope that millions of women needed to be able to access if required on Friday evening before going out for the night.

Or what about Progressive Insurance with its message: "We don't

> sell insurance; we sell speed." Not obviously a winner for an insurance company you might think. Until you hear the stories about the company from people who have dealing with it.
>
> One driver who lived in Dallas, drove from Dallas to see family in Kansas City one Christmas, and then on the way back decided to pay a visit to some relatives in St Louis. On the way through St. Louis, though, they were involved in a multi vehicle pile up, fortunately escaping with just a few scratches to the rear of the car. So after exchanging insurance details, they proceeded on their way back to Dallas, arriving at around midnight and crashing into bed.
>
> The next morning, eight o'clock in the morning, there is a bang, bang, bang downstairs. A man from Progressive Insurance is at the door. The first instinct is, sorry but we do not need any insurance. But then the man says that he is there about the accident the night before. The driver that caused the accident was insured by Progressive, the insurance man has already assessed the damage on the car in the drive. He tells the driver of the damaged car to take it the dealership and get it fixed, and hands over a cheque; and if it is more then they will pay up 20% extra.
>
> And suddenly "we sell speed," makes sense.

So the starting point for framing a debate is not just about what is going to work in the marketplace in the shot term; it is actually a business planning process rather than a marketing exercise. Usually marketing and communication come further down the line, with the organisational conversation about framing taking place first.

Framing, therefore, sets out the space that you want to operate in either as an individual, or as an organisation, and you come up with a framing message, principally a core proposition that sets that out.

For example, way back in its corporate history Nokia was a successful company in the timber business, it also made rubber boots. Then, in 1992, CEO Jorma Ollila emerged from a brainstorming session with a new frame of reference "Telecom-oriented, global focus, value-added". Through the latter part of the 1990s and the early part of this century Nokia has redefined itself as a mobile phone manufacturer.

Now, however, Nokia is once again in the process of reframing the space that it wants to operate in. "Today, the Internet is Nokia's quest," announces its website, supported by the message "Nokia is the world leader in mobility, driving the transformation and growth of the converging Internet and communications industries."

So Nokia has shifted its frame of reference to connectivity and the web, and in doing so marshalled its consumers in that direction too. Of course it takes a bit of clout to make such a major shift. As a market leader with a substantial share of the handheld market, Nokia should be able to successfully drive the market forward mapping out is future success by redefining itself not in terms of handheld devices, but in terms of access, and connecting consumers to the Internet, and by extension associating itself with the successful vision of the future embraced by companies such as Facebook and Google. A classic example of thought leadership at work.

So framing is not really about spin; it is about really going back to the core of what makes you, as an individual or as a business, successful. Is that sustainable going forward? If it is not, try and establish a new playing field that you can move towards, and then develop the messages that support and help delineate that reframing. So, for example, players in the oil industry use the message "exploring for energy", rather than "drilling for oil", shifting the debate and recruiting stakeholders to create a much more sustainable proposition for the organisation.

Reframe the market

A framing exercise can have wide repercussions, affecting entire markets, rather than just the immediate organisation doing the framing.

Ryanair, the budget airline, is a good example of how an organisation framed its space in such a way that it shifted the rules of the entire market, and in such a way that suited Ryanair better than the competition.

The Ryanair proposition focused on price. The situation in the European market at the time Ryanair entered the market was predominately one of premium airlines operating in short and medium haul. When Ryanair started flying to short and medium haul, it championed the message that flying could be cheap, and began relentlessly pushing prices down.

Now, by establishing the frame that flying could be cheap and then validating that, he began a journey which has been successful for him, but also shifted the rules of the game for the competition as well.

First Ryanair took on the state-run organisation which was charging a standard fare, the same as British Airways or other non-budget airlines might do. One of the most profound effects of Ryanair's reframing exercise was that AerLingus has had to reframe itself as a low fares airline. Aer Lingus now competes directly on price with Ryanair and has adopted many of the same modus operandi as Ryanair.

So the proposition around making flying cheap, which Ryanair needed to be validated in order for it to continue on an ongoing basis, not only pushed Ryanair's consumer proposition forward, but changed the rules of the game, brought state owned organisations, such as Aer Lingus, completely around to its way of thinking, and also generated competition such as EasyJet.

Room for manoeuvre

Organisations need to be careful when undertaking a framing exercise, as it is possible to create problems in the future, by leaving the organisation with little room for manoeuvre.

With Ryanair, for example, because it is so focused on its frame, which is making flying cheap, it has got very little space for manoeuvre – it lives and dies on the cheapness of its fares. So when, for example, the price of fuel starts go up, it becomes less cheap, although it is certainly cheaper than others, and then it may have to change its proposition.

So, to a degree, the singularity of focus of the frame has been incredibly successful for Ryanair, and yet at the same time left the company no room for manoeuvre. Consequently, the company is beginning to draw some criticism from consumer associations for charging for other elements of the flight, possibly in an effort to keep the basic price and the company's central proposition, down.

So, for example, it has introduced a new initiative of charging €6 per credit card booking per passenger, per leg. That is actually a substantial amount of money and has been criticised in some quarters, not least because it seems slightly more complicated way of charging for the tickets.

Comparing Ryanair's difficulties with Virgin is instructive. Virgin Atlantic's operations have also become more expensive due to the inexorable increase in the price of fuel. However, Branson framed Virgin's proposition as making flying fun, rather than making flying cheap, and so Virgin has more room for manoeuvre on price variability than Ryanair.

In practice

The framing concept may sound easy, and the end result needs to be simple, clear and contain some wisdom within it, yet framing is not that easy because, particularly within an organisation, there is so much complexity, so much process, that it is very hard for the organisation to align itself around a clear and simple proposition.

In many ways meeting the framing challenge is more a function of leadership than management, because the framing sets the agenda and tone for the organisation, so it is about leading the way forward, and involves inspiration and vision.

In practice the framing exercise will often be an external facilitated session with expert consultants to help the organisation understand where it needs to move with its stakeholders in order to continue to be successful. The people in the organisation are pushed towards a point of clarity and simplicity regarding what the organisation is about, either in terms of its overall purpose, or what it feels about particular issues.

All change

With all the talk of framing and messages moving stakeholders from one place to another in terms of behavioural change, you might be tempted to ask what happens with messages that do not require your audience to do something in particular.

In reality, however, there are few messaging situations that do not require action of some sort. Even if you have a message which is asking the consumer to do nothing different, the context and environment in which you are doing business is usually changing. So you may be asking the audience to stick with you in a changing world.

In truth when you look at executives in the workplace, and businesses in their own marketplace, there are really no examples these days of those executives and businesses not undergoing a radical challenge to what they are doing. So when you take any organisation that appears not change very often, in fact it is constantly being challenged from all directions.

Take the car park business. At first sight, could there be a less dynamic, unchanging business? You get a piece of waste land, either underground or over ground, you build a car park, people park their cars, and you charge them for the pleasure.

YOU'VE BEEN FRAMED

> **Message memo: Framing the debate**
>
> Just as you can have framing issues that relate to an organisation's core business purpose so to you can have a framing proposition around a specific debate. So it might be, for example, if you are a food retailer, what your game plan is for the future with regard to genetically modified food.
>
> In large parts of Europe, including the UK, genetically modified food is seen as a bad thing, for a variety of reasons, not least the fear that genetically modified food may have an adverse long term impact. So instinctively people do not trust corporations on this subject. As a result, many governments and retailers have agreed not to allow genetically modified crops to be grown, and not to sell products that contain genetically modified foodstuffs.
>
> However, a new issue has arisen regarding the increasing cost of food, both for developing and developed nations. It may well be that the only solution to rising food process is through non-organic food, and in particular by increasing yields and productivity through genetic modification.
>
> Consequently as a retailer, it may be time to reframe the debate over genetically modified foodstuffs to assert that genetic modification has a role to play in our diet because it allows food to remain affordable, and that such products will be offered to the public.

Examine the business more closely and it is soon apparent that many large car park businesses are part of listed companies. These companies are on a relentless drive for double digit growth. With a finite number of parking spaces, and market forces restricting the amount that can be charged, car parks are not an obvious source of double digit growth, so something more is required.

The solution lies in reframing. The growth for car parking organisations lies not in the provision of car parks, but in a move to overall parking solutions. When you move from the provision of car parks to providing parking solutions you have shifted the debate, the organisational agenda, from the finite physical geopolitics of providing physical space, towards the overall issue of parking provision.

In practice, that means that the car parking firms can now get contracts from local councils to start sending traffic wardens out and giving people tickets. That is a big shift in a business that does not at first sight seem faced with radical change.

So in many businesses where a first reaction might be to think that it is an unchallenged area, in reality it is emphatically radically challenged, whether it is because of the digital world, or because of the macrotrends such as the cost of fuel rising or food increasing.

On a personal note

Framing is not just for organisations. It is also equally effective for individuals, conveying messages. To a degree, framing is associated directly with values that have currency within an organisation and with the organisation's frame of reference. But on a personal level, framing also is very important, because for people to be successful in progressing within an organisation, they need to find their own frame of reference that fits with the objectives of the organisation.

Over the last decade an increase in outsourcing by organisations has meant a steady trickle of job losses. In times of economic turbulence, such as the world is experiencing with the credit crunch, that trickle is likely to become a flood. Restructuring, reengineering, reorganising, whatever you want to call it, for the employee it means insecurity and possible redundancy.

Framing can, however, help employees reduce the odds of being canned in the next round of layoffs. How? By using framing to help understand what value they contribute to the organisation. Note that is not what value you used to represent to the organisation, because businesses do not look backwards; they are always looking forward to the next quarter, the next year.

When you are using framing at a personal level, you need to consider what organisational values you can be associated with. There are usually two or three dominant values in an organisation at any point in time – you can probably find them listed on the corporate website.

As the CEO travels around the organisation, explaining the new vision and mission, part of your framing process must be to recognise where you can directly align what you do at work with the organisation's values. How do your day-to-day or ancillary activities, enable the organisation's frame of reference

A good example of this is Y2K and the millennium bug, which was supposed to cause a computer melt-down when the computer clocks changed to 2000. The framing value, for organisations, was "be prepared." The people who did very well promotion wise from Y2K showed themselves to be rainmakers for Y2K preparedness. These people joined Y2K action committees, took time off over the holiday period to come into work and to make sure the organisation was prepared for Y2K transition.

That was not just a technical enterprise. It was a way of allying to the new value in the organisation – "be prepared" – and treating that as an opportunity for self promotion. Many people in IT got on the promotion radar through their Y2K work and made rapid progress within the organisation when the year change had passed.

Because then you are valuable to the organisation; it is directly associated with your ability to command and budget on resource as well. And the allocations for wanting to get prepared were extraordinary, to a billion dollars were prepared for Y2K and so forth.

So framing for the individual is classically this: to survive and thrive going forward in the organisation, to get promoted, to get that pay rise, become associated with emerging values in the organisation, either proactive ones –about driving the organisation forward, or defensive ones which are around maintaining the status quo, such as cost reduction. And you need to be doing this besides doing accounts, marketing or whatever your normal role in the enterprise is.

GET THE MESSAGE

- Framing is not about spin.

- It is about being realistic about where you can lead people; acknowledging strengths and weaknesses and shifting the debate accordingly.

- Take care not to lose the audience when changing frames.

- Try to leave room for manoeuvre, otherwise you may find the frame you choose can be limiting or cause you problems in the future.

- Be aware that your reframing exercise may alter the behaviours of your competitors by redefining the market that you operate in.

- Framing can also be a very powerful tool to help maximise personal performance and achieve personal goals.

NINE

Messages as Conversations and Transactions

Conversations are the building-blocks of communication. They are everywhere. They are how we transmit information and feelings. They are also how we make sense of the world and the people in it. They are how we make and keep friends.

What, you might ask, have conversations got to do with organisational messaging? In the past organisations put their messages out without any expectation, or even desire, for interaction with their audience. Today the situation is different. Consumers are far more active, for a start. As are other stakeholders. The interactivity of the internet means that organisations now have to engage with their audience, and to do this well they need to understand the mechanics of conversation and dialogue.

Competition is much tougher for organisations today too. So when your competitors decides it would be a good idea to encourage feedback from stakeholders and act upon it in a way that allows them to improve their performance, and their products and services, then you need to encourage feedback, and act upon it too, if you were not already.

Equally it is no longer effective in most organisations to manage from the top down in an autocratic way. Instead you need to be participatory, collaborative and understand how dialogue works.

There is a need, therefore, to understand, conversations a little better, so that they can be put them to more effective use as a means of conducting business messages.

It takes two, baby

The world of theatre may be full of soliloquies, where the actor or actress stands on the stage, alone, talking to themselves, or at the audience, but in real life a conversation usually involves two or more consenting individuals. There are those that regularly engage in a dialogue with themselves — usually an internal dialogue. And there are those that joke they are the only person that they can have a sensible conversation with, which some may find amusing, but is unfortunately an attitude many organisations and managers have held for far too long.

So what is a conversation? Although they are everyday occurrences that we are all accustomed to, conversations are not to be taken for granted. They are quite complex and interesting events, and something that organisations and individuals would benefit from taking a closer look at.

We can start by considering what a conversation is not. A

MESSAGES AS CONVERSATIONS AND TRANSACTIONS

conversation is not a meaningless string of words or sounds. It should be based on an exchange of verbal signifiers, "words" that is, which carry meaning. Conversations are opportunities for information exchange, from the practical, "our product is good for doing this," to the subjective "but we think your product is also good for doing that." Conversations are also a means of making sense of the world around us and establishing meaningful social relations, as the countless Facebook members and visitors to the Internet's many chat rooms will know.

A very, very, brief history of conversations

The art of conversation has been around for a long time, as long as language has been invented, not that it was always given that name. In fact, the word "conversation" is a comparatively recent introduction to the lexicon, and used to have a number of meanings.

Up until the time of the Renaissance in the 1400s, "conversation" was used in a range of circumstances: it meant a manner of living, or behaviour; a transformational process; living with someone— and not necessarily talking to them. In late Medieval Latin "conversatio stomachii" meant digestion.

Interestingly conversation also had some connotations that, while not the meaning ascribed to the word today, are still very relevant to messaging. So, for example, it could refer to the act of conversion to a faith or creed, thus Saul's change of direction on the road to Damascus was termed "Conversatio Sancti Pauli." It is an appropriate meaning of the word, in the context of modern communication, when the role of the message is to seek to covert the audience to a cause and course of action.

But it was only in the sixteenth century that the word took on its familiar meaning in the English language of a verbal discourse. And then two centuries later the term was popularised when English ladies and gentlemen embarked on their Grand Tour of cultural Europe, brought back the Italian fashion for conversaziones – a particular gathering where social and intellectual exchanges took place.

It is noticeable that the conversation has long been claimed by the literati, as a cut above the slightly vulgar "chat", and there are those that lament the dying of the art of conversation. The truth is that, regardless of the reasons for doing it, everyone, the poor, the rich, the intellectual and the ignorant, converse. However, as we will see, and organisations and individuals need to appreciate, not everyone converses in the same way.

Just what is a conversation?

In the late '60s sociologists in the US, like Harvey Sachs, began to focus their attention on conversations. They began to analyse them, not in terms of the content and what people were talking about, but instead about how people talked. How long did people talk for? Did they "hand over the microphone" in an orderly fashion, or were they interrupted by someone else seizing the conversational initiative? How long did it take for someone to butt in? Were conversations orderly affairs, with conversational rules, as in sport, or were they free-for-alls?

What the sociologists discovered should inform organisations that engage in dialogues with their audiences, such as the increasingly popular Internet mediated Q&A sessions, as it revealed a complex

MESSAGES AS CONVERSATIONS AND TRANSACTIONS

but essential set of unspoken characteristics and rules that define and govern effective conversations.

A conversation is based around an often complex system of turn taking. A and B decide to have a chat. A talks about a subject, maybe at length, but then at some point stops talking, offering B the opportunity to respond. At this point B is being handed the microphone. Allowing B to contribute to the conversation after an appropriate moment denotes a fair and reasonable approach to the communication process on the part of A. It is an opportunity for B to agree with A, to tell him that he is wrong, or maybe to change the topic of conversation.

Some people fail to understand the rules of conversational engagement even at this basic level, and will continue on without respite. This is viewed as bad conversational manners and will not be regarded favourably by a modern audience. So remember to create opportunities for the audience to join in on the conversation.

Conversations can be of the simple question and response type.
    A. Have you tried our new yoghurt?
    B. Yes I have.

These can be drawn out a bit but not indefinitely.
B could say "Yes I have. It's very nice? Are you doing any new flavours?" and A could respond that although they are not at present, they do have plans for more.

Another type of conversation works on embedded questions and answers, each one dependant on a response but not independent.

THE MESSAGE

A. Have you spoken with Peter yet?
B. Is he here?
A. Haven't you see him then?
B. No, not yet. Why?
A. Well he's in the pub over the road, telling everyone who'll listen what a lousy company he works for.
B. Oh dear. I haven't been in there.

So conversations are made up of words strung together to give meaning. They have structure, and as we will see, they also have rules.

In the 1950s and '60s American philosopher Herbert Grice took a hard look at conversation. His conclusion was that it was full of implications or implicatures. These were implied assumptions made about the content of a conversation. Taken as a whole these added up to conversation axioms; unspoken rules underlying discourse. They help us to cut corners, to not have to spell everything out. Most people accept them and internalise them. They are conventions which everyone signs up to due to what Grice called the "co-operative principle". They help people to co-operate and enhance mutual comprehension.

According to Grice there are four maxims, or rules of conversation.

- *The maxim of quality*. A person is expected not to tell downright lies, or offer opinions for which they have no evidence.

- *The maxim of quantity*. A person is expected neither to give too much nor too little factual information.

- *The maxim of relation.* The person is assumed not to say things which are irrelevant.

- *The maxim of manner.* The person is always expected to be brief, well-ordered in their speech and never to waffle on endlessly.

- *The maxim of continuity.* This is an extension of the maxim of relation. Essentially when two (or more) people are talking about a topic, none of the participants will unilaterally start talking about a different, unrelated topic without signalling the change of direction in some way.

So, for example, a business might have a sign up in its stores saying, "End of season sale. Massive reductions. Up to 80% off." But, after the shoppers have queued up for the sale and finally get in through the store doors, they discover that only one item has 80% off, and everything else has 25% or less off. Now strictly speaking the statement is accurate, as there is "up to" 80% off one selected item, however, the statement is an inadequate because it gives too little information.

The majority of consumers will enter the sales expecting significant reductions, more than just the one item at 80%. Consequently on finding out the truth, they will probably feel cheated, especially if they are regular customers that value the brand. The organisation should have known the truth, and, if adhering to the maxim of quantity, it should have given an adequate representation of it.

Perhaps the most important of the maxims in a business context is the maxim of quality. This is a big problem for message senders, whether in business or politics. Unfortunately the quality of messages emanating from organisations and individuals has deteriorated over recent years, leaving a highly sceptical public doubting the truth of many messages. Politicians and journalists are probably the least believed, but many corporations are not far behind.

Claims to be environmentally friendly are a good example; nine out of ten delegates and participants that attended the 2007 UN Climate Change Conference at Bali believed companies are guilty of "greenwashing," — misleading consumers regarding the environmental practices of a company or the environmental benefits of a product or service — according to a survey conducted by EnviroMedia Social Marketing.

Events like those involving the Hungarian prime minister in 2006, do not help matters. In late 2006, the Hungarian prime minister was taped making an injudicious speech to party insiders. He stated that his government had done nothing for years and that it had lied through its teeth to get re-elected. Thousands of angry Hungarians took to the streets demanding the premier's resignation, but many people could not see what the fuss was about. They rationalised their sang-froid by saying "So he lied, but that's what politicians do."

Conversations, then, must be underpinned by trust if the messages imparted are to be effective. And this means focusing on the maxim of quality – do not tell lies or half-truths, do not be disingenuous, do not be economical with the actualité. You can do a lot to make messages in your conversations stickier by working on the maxims of manner, maybe of relativity as well, but unless you establish a channel of trust you might as well be shouting down a disconnected telephone line.

MESSAGES AS CONVERSATIONS AND TRANSACTIONS

Silence please

The rules of conversations are culturally dependent. In the world of business, board meetings are structured according to the "ideal" conversation, for example. One person has the floor and has to be heard out, without interruption. Yet this is culture specific. North Americans are often considered to be less restrained. They will jump in when they have something, anything, to say. This can lead to unfortunate and unfavourable stereotyping.

Let's return to the two conversationalists A and B. A has spoken at some length about something, and then decides to let B have a go, so he stops talking. In many cultures not only does B now have the right to speak, he also has an obligation to speak. If he says nothing it will certainly not go unobserved. Usually though B makes some sort of sound and is rarely completely silent. Why? Because overlong silence is usually considered awkward and embarrassing during a conversation.

The discomfort felt at periods of lengthy silence during a conversation may relate to basic personal security. When we encounter people that are new to us we want to be able to assess quickly whether they are a friend or foe. The answer can be obtained fairly quickly by attempting conversation. If the person engages in conversation they are less likely to be an enemy. We use conversation to establish relationships, even of the most trivial kind.

A conversation is a series of messages, but it is not a one-way process. It is something that everyone can and should participate in. A real and effective conversation is never a dialogue des sourdes – a dialogue of the deaf. The other person must be listened to.

THE MESSAGE

Message memo: Cultural misunderstandings

The cultural context of conversations is imperative to a proper communications interchange.

Take the members of the Navajo and Apache nations in the American south west. Unlike people in many other cultures, for the Navajo and Apache, idle chit-chat is not a convenient ice breaker for conversational purposes; they only speak when they have got something important to say. Speculating about the weather, or the bonus features of a particular product, such conversational triviality would be viewed with disdain.

Unsurprisingly when these Native Americans come together with other cultures which view any topic as fair game for conversation, then misunderstandings can and do occur.

Misunderstandings like those encountered by the Europeans when they first ventured into British Columbia, Canada, home to the Athabaskans at the time.

The Athabaskans have a similar attitude to trivial conversations as the Navajo and Apache. Moreover, when they are unsure about the appropriateness of establishing contacts, even at the level of the conversational, their response is usually to stay silent. They have to be fairly confident of who they are talking to and what they are talking about to join in a conversation.

When the Europeans met the Athabaskans they were invariably the first to speak. Then they went on and on, often about little things. The Athabaskans, who understood them perfectly, were a little taken aback. They were not sure whether verbal communications with these strangers was appropriate, so they kept silent, even when the Europeans stopped and indicated it was the Athabaskan's turn to speak. The Europeans, discomforted by the silence, started talking again.

Consequently, the conversational exchanges were one-sided. The two groups were then asked what they thought of each other based on these encounters. The Europeans couldn't make up their minds about the Athabaskans. They seemed shy, but also quite haughty and surly. The Athabaskans considered the Europeans to be rude, garrulous and domineering.

Some cultures consider silence, or lack of conversation, to be the norm during certain activities. Any visitor to Scandinavia who has ever been fortunate enough to get invited to a dinner party in Finland soon notices one thing. While the food is invariably delicious, it is consumed by all in almost silence. No small-talk. Eating is a serious activity. This can cause deep discomfort for non-Finns unused to silent mealtimes.

Cultural conflicts can also stymie conversations within a culture, between rich and poor, old and young, even between male and female. The American socio-linguist Dorothy Tannen demonstrated in her book You Just Don't Understand that men and women have different ways of participating in a conversation. Failure to recognise this causes tension.

What these cultural misunderstandings emphasise is the need for organisations and individuals to appreciate the cultural sensitivities of the audience that they are conversing with. Otherwise the messages may well be ineffective, even counterproductive.

THE MESSAGE

Sure, the importance of listening to the customer has been preached eloquently for years: it is part of Management by Walking Around, postulated by US management guru Tom Peters among others. But it has to be about more than a clickable link at the bottom of a web page labelled "feedback". We have to see customers in a new light, maybe not as an audience to be entertained but as a community to serve.

And who is our community? It is any company's stakeholders, not just present ones, but also those it is likely to acquire. A business's community is anyone likely to be affected (hopefully beneficially) by the business's operations. The conversations with this community have to be on-going, 24/7, 365 days a year.

Going back to the earlier meaning of conversation, it involves a cohabitation with this community, actually living and breathing in it. Corporate organisation will have to respond to this environment by appointing a Community Liaison director, but this won't be just another functional silo with its own discreet budget and rules of engagement. Community Liaison must run throughout the organisation.

If an organisation enters into a dialogue with its stakeholders, it cannot afford to withdraw from that conversation if the stakeholders are unexpectedly critical of the organisation, for example. Too often business pays lip-service to customer feedback.

A start can be made by remembering that effective communication depends on seeing the whole process at first as a transaction. You have something you want to give. The success of the transaction depends on the other person taking it. They may not like it, or even know what to do with it, but it's important to establish the transfer

Message memo: Community spirit

One social tool that organisations are increasingly turning to, and individuals becoming involved in, is the online community. It is a forum where careful messaging is essential to maintain the integrity of the community.

At Cass Business School in the city of London, Caroline Wiertz, a senior lecturer in marketing, has conducted some interesting research into the effective use of online communities.

Online communities used by organisations come in two main types, says Wiertz. One is brand focused, and a highly effective tool for customer relationship management, product feedback, relationship building and market intelligence. A good example is the Harley Davidson Owners Group, bringing brand enthusiasts together to discuss the products, plus various other social activities, some Harley related, some not.

The other type of community is the service support, problem solving community. Cost savings are a key driver here – it is cheaper for a company to host an online community than host a call centre or send out a service technician.

Creating a successful community is not easy, however. While the technology underpinning online communities is well proven, with plenty of choice in the market, there are tough challenges associated with managing such a community.

it is the social interaction that holds the community together, and the importance of social interaction grows over time. The host

> organisation must also allow for social integration, that means tolerating, even encouraging, non-product related interaction. So organisations should not send out the message that are going to be over controlling.
>
> Organisations must not underestimate the commitment and responsibility that running an online community or social network involves. There have been instances, for example, where companies have pulled an online community without discussion, and the consequent consumer backlash has dented profits.

transaction for your message. Even rejection is better than being ignored – ask any speed-dater. Rejection is something that can be worked with. Eventually your message is taken on board. The more times the message transaction is repeated, the more trust is established. Eventually the transaction framework dissolves, leaving behind a communications channel.

So remember, messaging is about conversations, not soliloquies, it is about talking with, not at people, it is about participation.

GET THE MESSAGE

- Conversations are the building blocks of conversation; they are about exchanges, two or many way transactions.

- Researchers have discovered that conversations are

MESSAGES AS CONVERSATIONS AND TRANSACTIONS

governed by a complex but essential set of unspoken characteristics and rules.

- There are four maxims of conversations: quality; quantity; relation; and manner. (And one extra – continuity – which is an extension of relation).

- You need to understand the role and importance of silence in conversations.

- Cultural misunderstandings are common, and need to be avoided. So be aware the cultural sensitivities of the audience in terms of conversation rules.

TEN

Seeking Inspiration?

In this chapter we are going to discuss inspiration, an essential component of many messages. In doing so the main focus is on speaking, and presentations of one type or another, where the speaker is visible to some people at least – even if the others are only able to hear the audio. So less about the written message, although inspiration can be important in this context too.

And where better to start than the inspirational lecture delivered by the late Randy Pausch, professor of Computing at Carnegie Mellon University in the US. Having been diagnosed with terminal cancer Pausch gave a talk to students at the University as part of a lecture series at the University. The subject of the lecture was Pausch's childhood dreams.

The presentation earned Pausch unintentional global fame, as the simple, humorous, but deeply powerful talk inspired millions of people around the globe who watched via YouTube or Google Video clip.

We would encourage anybody that wants to understand how to

THE MESSAGE

inspire an audience to watch Pausch's lecture, there is no doubt that whatever culture you are from or area of business or social life you operate in, there will be something for you learn in terms of understanding inspirational speaking.

Clarity, simplicity

One reason that the lecture Pausch gives is so powerful is that his serious condition leads him to strip the contents of his talk to the bare essentials. The starting point is that people are witnessing something that is actually both simple but also quite profound and clear as well.

When we look at what inspires people, clarity and simplicity are very important. Artifice must be stripped away revealing the very essence of the person delivering the message. People that are genuinely inspiring are often able to communicate during different, often difficult, challenging situations, yet maintain their personal integrity, and at the same time connect with many people, transcending barriers.

Inspiro

When you are looking for the source of inspiration, it is tempting to start looking outward; to think that those people who inspire have an ability to project externally. We believe, however, that the starting point is actually the opposite perspective, looking inward.

The origin of the word inspiration is "inspiro," from the Greek to breathe in, and to a degree that sense of taking in air, or breathing

SEEKING INSPIRATION?

in, is the starting point of your journey to be an inspiring communicator.

So inspiring people, do light up the room, or lecture hall, they may generate great admiration within their community or across the world, but the starting point is internal, something within themselves that they use to drive their message forward.

Nature or nurture

Can anyone be inspirational? It is easy to understand why some people might believe only certain special individuals are able to inspire others. But if it is a question nature versus nurture then we would argue that most people are capable of being inspirational.

All that is needed is to be able to search inside yourself for that starting point and then ally that to your cause, whether it is recruiting employees, or promoting some aspect of corporate and social responsibility. So inspiration is partly innate but partly a function of practice and experience.

Qualities of inspiration: the characteristics of the inspirational individual

In many of the workshops that we have run around the world, we asked people to characterise the attributes of the inspiring individual. Obviously a number of different characteristic were identified, but three in particular kept cropping up: passion, charisma and credibility.

Passion

What do you care about deeply as an individual, or as a leader? What are the things in your business life, your work life, your social life, and your sporting or cultural life that you really value? If you look through your life to actually find those elements, you can discover a touchstone to help you inspire others.

So you need to consider what it is that you genuinely care about, whether it is your family, jazz music, or the football team you support. It may well be something that has nothing to do with what you want to talk about, but that you are passionate about. It does need to be appropriate, however, some subjects are not the stuff of inspirational speeches, no matter how passionately you feel about them.

The next step is to make connections between your passions and the cause that you are promoting whether it is a business objective, or a personal cause. Then you can capture that sense of genuine drive, excitement, energy, enthusiasm, and humanity, and use that to make your message more inspirational.

Injecting passion into your messages is something that everybody can do, because everybody has got something that they really care about.

Charisma

Charisma is the second characteristic that people commonly associate with inspiring individuals. You might think that of all the characteristics, charisma really is something that people innately possess, you either have it or you do not. That charismatic people just walk into a room and light it up, because that is the way that they are, and it is not something that can be taught.

SEEKING INSPIRATION?

Here, though, we would have to disagree. Question people more thoroughly about what charismatic actually means to them, and you will get answers that talk about connection and confidence. If passion is about inspiro, looking inwards and drawing on something within, charisma is about looking outwards, reaching and connecting.

While some speakers are naturally charismatic, and we have witnessed this kind of charisma at first hand, others attain charisma through hard work and practice.

The non verbal aspects of communication are very important in creating charisma. The firm handshake, with the second hand touching the extended arm of the person you are greeting, looking someone in the eye, the confident erect posture, clear vocal delivery with no mumbling, smiling, warmth; these are all part of being charismatic. Equally, charisma is about finding common ground, finding a point of common connection and recognising that, it is about active listening and empathy, seeing the world through other people's eyes, but also about control.

Whether or not you appear charismatic, will also depend on other factors such as what you wear, your surroundings and the way that other people treat you. Factors like dress and surroundings may become less important as you master the art of being charismatic, but they will certainly be part of creating an overall impression to begin with.

Remember too that you cannot fake connection or confidence, you must believe, because if you do not believe, your audience never will.

Credibility

Finally, the third characteristic that comes up in conversations about inspiration most frequently is credibility. Credibility is about trust. In turn, trust is not something that can be forced; a good starting point is trusting other people and reaching out to them, to build a two-way bridge.

Credibility is also to do with competence; not over promising and not mismanaging people's expectations. Under promise, over deliver is a maxim worth having in mind in your business and personal dealings, including any messages that you create.

As part of developing your credibility credentials you need to be clear about direction, it is good to be empathetic, but you must still be focused on your cause.

Humility is also important. The credible leader manager is one who cares about what they do, has a degree of technical competence, but are also candid about what they do not know. As Socrates says: "the only true wisdom is in knowing you know nothing".

We can't all be James Brown

There is a misconception that if we need to inspire somebody with what we do and say, then the best way of going about that is it to be like somebody who is already inspirational.

James Brown, the famous soul and funk singer, electrified his audience with all manner of thrills and spills and innovations in his shows. But while some entertainers have attempted to mimic the brilliant entertainer's showmanship, few have come close to capturing the magic of his performance.

SEEKING INSPIRATION?

The idea with inspiration, then, is not trying to copy other people, necessarily. Instead, you need to find your own voice and character, your own traits and idiosyncrasies, and use those as a basis for inspiration.

So, if you are a senior executive, rather than attempting to emulate Richard Branson, who has a unique inspirational style, you would be better advised to develop your own style. If you work in marketing, but have a colleague, who is inspirational in another function, do not try to copy their approach, but combine personal experiences and your knowledge of marketing to communicate in an inspirational way.

Whether you work in research and development, innovation, sales, marketing, or accounts, and even if you do not count yourself as particularly extrovert, high energy or actively engaging, you will be able to use your technical competence to inspire.

A case in point is one woman who was due to address European Union politicians on patient care, and it was the first time she had ever ventured outside of her own country, let alone to Brussels, and the European parliament. This woman was not overly extrovert and you would have been hard pressed to imagine her as a captivating, inspiring speaker.

However, what we did not know at the time was that this woman has also gone through some 25 years of difficulties regarding her health, tough problems. Her experiences, allowed her to find her own voice and perspective. When she told her story, about what she had been through, it was an electrifying experience, and incredibly inspiring.

Her powerful and inspirational message showed us that almost anybody can find their own voice and inspire, if they go about it in the right way. And, while you should be careful not to copy other inspirational people completely, it is a good idea to borrow one or two tricks of the trade, while retaining your own personality.

Tapping into your own personal journey

Not everyone finds it easy to tap into their own personal journey, but there are some practical methods that you can use that will help. We are not saying the process will be easy, but it will be effective.

One starting point is to enlist good friends and close colleagues, and conduct your own informal 360º feedback exercise. The 360 is a common way of assessing people in organisations, by asking other people that you work with, both those you manage and those that manage you, how you operate in the organisation.

The idea here is to conduct the same exercise informally. Ask a range of people who know you well, friends, family, work colleagues, to describe you in writing or verbally, listing both the positives and negatives, and you should get a reasonably candid assessment of your strengths and weaknesses.

Once you have the results back, pay attention to what people say, and do not dismiss it because it doesn't accord with the way that you see yourself. Do not be surprised, either, if the way other people see you, differs considerably from your own view of your strengths and weaknesses and the way that you operate. You may consider yourself a quiet person, while others say that when you are talking about a subject that you obviously care about, you become much more extrovert.

Look at the adjectives that people use to describe you, listen to what

SEEKING INSPIRATION?

people tell you, and be open to the critique that is implicit in an exercise like 360º feedback. This is a very good starting point to begin to learn about yourself, and to develop some more self-awareness. The listening aspect of this is a very useful exercise in itself, because the people who are often able to persuade most effectively, are often those people who have excellent listening skills.

As well as the informal exercise you can also benefit from any similar assessment devices used within the organisation, so be sure to take full advantage of these, rather than seeing them as some sort of ordeal or chore.

Myers Briggs

Another way of working out where you get your energy from, what kind of style suits you best, what your preference is when it comes to the way you engage with people, and so on, is the Myers Briggs personality test.

The test is based on the work of Swiss psychologist Carl Jung who developed a theory of personality based on eight personality types: extroverts, introverts, thinking, feeling, sensing, intuitive, judging and perceptive.

The Myers-Briggs Type Indicator was created in the 1970s by Isabel Briggs Myers. Supposedly, each individual has a principal way of operating with respect to: our flow of energy; how we take in; how we make; the every day lifestyle we lead. Within each of these categories we prefer to be: Extraverted or Introverted; Sensing or Intuitive; Thinking or Feeling; Judging or Perceiving. You can take the test, or instrument as they call it, online.

Message memo: Are you listening?

If you are inclined to butt in during conversations, or have a habit of talking over people, heed the words of Epictetus, a Stoic philosopher from Ancient Greece, who gave some useful advice on effective communication: "We have two ears and one mouth so that we can listen twice as much as we speak".

A job advertisement listed the following as a key criterion: "Demonstrated capacity to model active listening, strategic questioning and motivational techniques." So what is active listening?

When you are talking to someone, watch out for the person who repeats what you say, demonstrating in a subtle way to you that they are listening; who offers attentive nods and throws in an occasional "yes". They are probably studied in the art of active listening.

Active listening has its origins in the work of US psychologist Carl Rogers. There are several different techniques employed in active listening. One is to encourage the speaker. This can be through body language cues such as nodding or mirroring posture, through speech such as encouraging statement, "go on", "yes". Sometimes encouragement in active listening may simply involve saying nothing and allowing the other person to express their emotions, without criticism or judgement.

Rogers said that active listening was an important way to bring about change in people. He suggested that the listener should look out for three things. First, they should listen not just to the words but try to get a sense of the emotional undercurrent. Second, they should try to respond to the emotional content if it seemed more important the

> words. Third, they should pay attention to the non-verbal cues.
>
> Reflecting is also an essential aspect of active listening. It involves recapping what the speaker has said so that they have time to consider their own words. Simply copying phrases is not sufficient. It is far better to rephrase what the speaker has said, but in fewer words.
>
> There are several advantages to active listening. It encourages people to listen to each other and think about meaning of what the other person is saying. It also encourages people to open up, and if the listener is attuned to the speaker they are more likely to reach an understanding.

Project your voice

There are other things that you can do to help improve your communications game, to help get that golf ball the extra 50 yards that makes the difference between winning and losing.

So, for example, somebody who is quiet and introspective, often their voice is also quiet. But there are techniques you can borrow to help project your voice more. We are not talking about shouting here, either, but about making your voice easier to hear. If you are going to establish your voice it needs to be clear and resonant. You can borrow techniques from the world of theatre and the world of projecting your voice which gives you much more control of the room, when you speak to people, they actually pay attention.

It is not that difficult to project your voice. If you told the majority of people that they needed to project their voice better, they would probably not have got a clue what to do.

But if you listen to somebody on a train when they are on their mobile phone, it is hard to get their voice out of your head, even though they are trying to whisper into their phone. The reason is that they are projecting their voice into the mobile phone because they are imagining the person they are talking to some distance away.

So we are projecting our voice frequently throughout the day, it is just that we are not conscious of it. There are many books on vocal coaching and speech training, and it is a good idea to invest in one, in the meantime though, in terms of projecting your voice, think mobile phone – imagine you are speaking into a phone to somebody and you will find that automatically, your voice changes gear and you are projecting your voice.

Now pause

Studying the speeches of inspirational speakers such as Winston Churchill and JFK, Nelson Mandela, or Theodore Roosevelt, a number of things stand out. One in particular is the technique of using pauses to heighten the effect of the speech.

Listening to some of the most iconic speeches ever made over the last 60 or so years, it is soon apparent that the pause is a technique that all the great speakers have in common.

It is possible that these inspirational figures naturally incorporated these breaks into their speeches. However, even if this is the case, a

SEEKING INSPIRATION?

learnt behaviour, it is definitely a method that you can learn and incorporate into presenting style.

Why are pauses so effective? Going back to the entomology of inspiration, inspiro is about drawing breath and when we take breath we pause. The momentary break in the flow of the speech, allows the audience to catch up and digest what is being said, it heightens the suspense and increases the power and impact of what is being said. This is often true even if the subject matter is fairly mundane. And the technique will certainly add some pep to business related messages.

So, next time that you are busy focusing on projecting your voice, and in full flow during a presentation, remember to have the confidence to be silent every so often.

Pictures and places

Another technique that great communicators use to inspire people is to use words to paint a picture for their audience. As Colin Powell retired US Army General and former US secretary for state once said "great leaders are almost always great simplifiers, who can cut through argument, debate, and doubt, to offer a solution everybody can understand."

One way to simplify things when you are delivering a message is to refer to pictures and places, so that people have something concrete that they can relate to. Even if it is an abstract subject, such as democracy, or freedom, or tolerance, you can paint a picture of that in action, as a way to inspire the audience.

Try and characterise where you would like to be, or where you would like people to move towards, by outlining what that vision looks like. By doing this you allow others to more actively share in that vision.

This was another commonality that we discovered when we looked at the speeches of the most inspiring speakers. Going back to JFK, for example, he painted a picture of an American on the moon within a few years, and in a very concrete way.

The point of this vision, however, was not about putting people on a small desolate chunk of rock with no atmosphere or value in terms of mineral resources, Kennedy was really using the journey to the moon to illustrate the ambition of America in a competitive environment, to outdo its superpower rival, the USSR. In painting this picture, Kennedy provided the rest of America with a visual symbol that would remind them of his personal vision most nights.

It also allowed people to incorporate that sense of ambition into their own lives, hence the saying "shooting at the moon", and at the same time identify with Kennedy's message.

Quietly effective

Just as an additional point, we have communication trained thousands of people. In our experience, the people who are the most engaging and impressive when standing up, are often not the ones who are the big initial presence in the room, the people who have a lot to say, the glitzy or the glamorous.

Instead, it is often the case that the quieter people who shun the limelight and prefer to get their heads down and get on with the

SEEKING INSPIRATION?

job, are more impressive when they get on to the subject they want to talk about, because they strip away the fluff and superfluous and get right down to their simple effective powerful message.

GET THE MESSAGE

- You can learn to be inspiring.

- Clarity and simplicity are a good starting point.

- To begin with look inwards for inspiration; rather than outwards.

- Three qualities of inspiration: passion, charisma, credibility. And you can learn to demonstrate all three.

- Try to create your own style, rather than copy the style of others.

- Tap into your personal journey to inspire others.

- Practice the practical stuff—voice projection, using pauses effectively, using pictures and places to bring messages alive.

ELEVEN

Personal Connections

If we want to engage with other people and get them to buy into our messages, it is important that we buy into those messages ourselves to start with. In the 21st century people no longer just buy products and services, they also buy people, and so on a personal level it is difficult to sell something to someone else if you do not buy into it yourself.

Differing levels of immersion

Buy in requires immersion in the content of the message. It is not enough, just to be a conduit, or channel for information. You cannot just pass things along.

Often middle managers, for example, will be part of a message delivery chain that starts further up the organisational chain, at head office say. In this situation there may be a temptation to think that you are just acting as the mouthpiece for the organisation, and that there is no need for you to get involved with the message, just to pass it on as it is.

But this passive approach is not good enough any more. Managers and leaders need to engage with the contents of the message. This is partly due to the increasing demand for authenticity that we referred to earlier in the book.

A big challenge then, is to engage on a personal level while at the same time remaining on message from a corporate perspective.

The cultural challenge

In different cultures there are differing levels of appetite to engage with corporate organisational content personally.

In some cultures, Japan for example, and even the UK, there is often a feeling that it is not necessary, desirable or easy to get personally involved in the corporate line. People feel uncomfortable engaging on a personal level. Instead it is much easier to not get their hands dirty or their emotions ruffled, pass a message on and remain disengaged.

Other cultures, perhaps in the United States, are happier to meld the personal with the corporate, for people to get stuck in and get personally excited. So in Western Europe phrases such as "I'm personally very excited about this," "I'm adrenalised by this," or "I want to reach out to people," might be considered over the top. Whereas in America, that sense of personally reacting to the message is a far more acceptable part of the delivery.

So before you go into a room and demonstrate authenticity and personal connection, you need to be aware of cultural differences, and to make sure that you are culturally and contextually sensitive.

PERSONAL CONNECTIONS

Be aware that there are barriers in some cultures, or there may not be such a strong appetite for demonstrable personal connection. So the tone of voice, the amount of technical detail you deploy, the whole way you have of speaking, that has got to be culturally in tune with the audience.

If you were presenting within the public sector in the United Kingdom, in the Civil Service, for example, and start declaring your personal biases, and regaling people with your personal family anecdotes, it might be seems as "not the done thing". However, we have seen the same approach work very well in other cultures, interpreting what one culture might see as schmaltzy as inspiring instead.

Or if you wanted to have a spokesperson in the Middle East or in Saudi Arabia, you wouldn't choose a woman to do it because they tend not to see women as figures of authority.

Failure to be sensitive to cultural nuances can lead to major problems. At best cultural ignorance will mean that you fail to connect with your audience, at worst, however, in some countries it could lead to you ending up in jail.

If you are culturally ignorant then there are many ways of finding out what is acceptable in different parts of the world. There are books on business etiquette in different parts of the world. You could run your plans for presenting a message, and how you relate to it personally, by some of your colleagues in different parts of the world – if you have them.

Unfortunately, all too often messages get beamed out from HQ, and passed down the line, without too much attention to the cultural perspective, and while that is changing, there is still a long way to go.

THE MESSAGE

Are you prepared to 'jump in'?

If you are not prepared to jump in and get personally connected, then you may not be the best person to deliver the message. The message may be a perfectly necessary, well-crafted message, with the right context, aimed at the right audience and with the right call to action, everything right but the messenger. In which case, you may want to get somebody else to deliver the message.

Unfortunately, abdicating responsibility for delivering a message sends out its own message. The reality is, you're communicating all of the time by dint of not communicating. Communication is something that we all do every day, as part of an organisation, and we all have responsibility to do it. Ask yourself, do you want to leave the process unmanaged, or do you want to help manage and control the communication process.

Close to the source

Why do we need to buy-in to the message? Because we are dealing with an increasingly discerning audience. Globalisation, the proliferation of digital media, the onslaught of blogging, the yearning for authenticity, these all mean that are fewer barriers between the people creating the message, whether it is an organisation, or an individual and the recipients of that message. There is much greater transparency.

As a result messengers need to be more connected with the message for the message to appear real and meaningful. If a person in California wants to know how the US troops are faring in the Middle East, then they no longer have to have the message translated to them through a comparatively neutral, and distanced medium like Fox TV or the Department of Defence, instead they can get news much more immediately, by reading the blogs of the soldiers on duty in the Middle East, and looking at the photos and video clips that those soldiers are taking and posting up.

This is the kind of "real" information that people crave in modern society. The message captured on a mobile phone and recorded by an individual soldier caught in the cross fire in Basra is going to be much more convincing than the aggregated perspective from the soldiers' bosses or from culturally biased TV stations.

In an organisational context people will tend to believe an off the record aside made by a manager more than an on the record statement delivered by the same manager. So when a manager that spends an hour delivering the received word on restructuring and then in 15 seconds, give a totally different view with an off the record comment or an aside, that is the message people tend to gravitate towards.

So the distinction between the passive and active message, the structured, acutely planned somewhat sterile message and the apparently spontaneous impulsive unsanctioned aside is much less than it ever has been. And this muddied distinction is something that you need to be aware of when creating messages and also when mediating and delivering them, as a messenger.

People buy people

While Hillary Clinton was busy attacking Obama, with her camp accusing him of, among other things, being inexperienced and using

THE MESSAGE

Message memo: Making an impact

A huge amount of impact in messaging is non-verbal. Imagine the executive that spend ages working on a PowerPoint presentation for a team meeting. The presentation is gorgeous, it looks great, and the messages are spot on, and it is distilled down from 100 bullet points to maybe four really essential points.

The executive has rehearsed the presentation, it looks great, he is confident of a good reception, he gets up on stage, and the rest of the team are already glancing at their watches and wondering when it is going to be over and done with.

The impatience of the team members has nothing to do with the PowerPoint content, nothing to do with the slides; it all comes down to presentation skill. And by presentation skill, it has less to do with what is on the slides or what is written in the speech. Instead it has to do with other factors like the ability of the person to move on the stage, the dress and clothes they are wearing, and a myriad of other small details.

The emotion actually counts for a large part of message decision-making. It takes fractions of a second to form an opinion and make a decision, so rational decision-making, for the most part, is largely an illusion. People buy diet soda because they get the message that it contains "zero calories". Therefore it is good for you if you are watching your weight.

In most cases it is an emotional purchase. Few people check out the small print on the back of the bottle or package to see what other contents are in the product, how much sugar, for example. It is the kind of information you would have to take into account in order to make a rational decision.

PERSONAL CONNECTIONS

> It is one of the reasons that when you are drafting or editing a press release, an employee communications email, or any other kind of written communication it is so important to focus on the first two or three lines. Because, all too often, if you do not catch the audience at that point, you will not catch them at all as they make an emotional, irrational decision based on those opening lines. Rational arguments get overtaken by superficial emotions.

empty rhetoric, Obama managed somehow to personify his campaign message: Change We Can Believe In. He did so through his appearance, through his youth, and notably, by appearing not to engage to the same extent, in the same kinds of critical campaigning, or lengthy and convoluted speeches.

So although Clinton delivered her speeches in a very technically accomplished manner, supported by numerous facts and figures, she struggled throughout to find her own message with commentators criticising her campaign for a lack of overarching theme. Obama self-evidently embodied his message of change from the establishment, so much so that he did not need to engage in lengthy and detailed rhetoric, but instead used simple direct phrases, such as that when addressing his audience in Houston, Texas following his win in Wisconsin; "Houston, we have lift off."

On the one side there is the classic example of the old economy method of delivering the message in the classically received way, setting it up, deploying it, and recruiting the grassroots movement. On the other side there is the new economy way, epitomised by Obama who far more obviously embodies his message. The result is that Clinton appeared more inauthentic and contrived. And it was noticeable that her campaign received one of its biggest boosts when she became visibly emotional, tears welling up, in New Hampshire.

Digital world looking for an analogue origin

The digital world allows many more ways of communicating, whether it is via YouTube videos, personal blogs, podcasting, or corporate websites. However, when the internet first began to gain traction as means of communication to a wider audience, the digital medium appeared innately impersonal.

This was partly due to technology limitation, such as bandwidth constraints, which meant that audio and video were not widely available as communication tools. But with advances in technology, and bandwidth no longer so much of an issue, use of the internet has undergone an interesting transformation. Today the digital world is being used to provide a more sophisticated way of storytelling, of reaching back to a story telling tradition (more about storytelling in Chapter 12).

So as well as the opinions and reviews, blogs, video clips, podcasting and other social networking Web 2.0 tools can be used to provide the intimate warmth and closeness that the Web 1.0 lacked. For example, many of the popular clips on You Tube show cameos and excerpts from a larger story whether it is someone's life story, or an organisational story. Remember then that passive communication in the Web 2.0 world is no longer effective, getting the message over needs to be done in a way that invokes the spirit of traditional story telling, but using modern technology

Message memo: Not so LonelyGirl15

If you want to get message to a large percentage of Generation Y, forget conventional, traditional media. Sure magazines, papers and television have their place, but the Internet is where you will really connect with Gen Y.

The rise of viral video websites like YouTube, Google video, and social networking sites like MySpace and Facebook, are indicative of where the marketing world is heading.

A good example of the ability of YouTube to reach millions of Gen target audience was the phenomenon that was Bree, a sixteen year old, home-educated, schoolgirl — otherwise known as Lonelygirl15. Millions tuned in to watch the shy but precocious girl, talk about a panoply of subjects including the Tolstoy principle, turtles, friend Daniel, Heisenberg's uncertainty principle, and Purple Monkey.

However, as the number of viewers climbed steadily, rumours surfaced that all was not as it should be in the lonelygirl universe. Conspiracists maintained that the slick editing and production values hinted at something more commercial than a teenager's amateur video diary.

Sure enough Bree was outed as the not so lonely Jessica Rose, 19, formerly of the New York Film Academy (LA branch), and the filmmakers, Californian based twenty somethings, Miles Beckett, Mesh Flinders, and Greg Goodfried signed with top Hollywood talent agents, Creative Artists Agency. The whole home video diary thing was a charade –albeit an extremely popular, and, for a time, convincing one.

> It is not the fact that someone produced a fake video – or series of videos – on YouTube that is so remarkable about the lonelygirl phenomenon though. The part of the story that demands the attention of marketers the world over was the consumer/audience response to unfolding events. Lonelygirl15 was for some time the all-time number one video channel on YouTube.

PERSONALLY CONNECTING IN PRACTICE

Knowing the importance of connecting personally with the message is one thing, but actually achieving that connection can be quite a challenge. In practice a number of factors are important.

Panhandling through your past

If we go back to the message triangle highlighted earlier in the book, one of the corners of the triangle is "the you".

So you use examples in messages to bridge to the audience. The examples you provide as part of the message support the message, help to give it structure, and help to connect the audience to the message, providing relevance. And by connecting yourself, the messenger, to the message, then you also provide passion and authenticity. As we discussed in the previous chapter it actually allows you to be more inspiring by demonstrating that personal connection.

So the question is, how do you do that? You need to go back and try

PERSONAL CONNECTIONS

and find parallels between your own background, your life, your stories, things that have happened to you as an individual, and the point you're trying to get across.

A good example is an executive we were working with, who worked in the chemical sector. We were talking about the chemical world and the issue of innovation in the chemical business-to-business arena, and it was coming across as rather dry.

When we asked the executive if there was anything that he had done in his life that illustrated some of the points he wanted to bring out, he went in to a room next door and came out with a singed picture of a skier which said something along the lines of "Thanks for the Gold", and then told us an interesting story.

One year he was on a skiing holiday in the late 1990s near to where the Winter Olympics were being held. The snow was very soft and the skiers were recording very slow times. The executive got talking to the skiers in the lodge who were saying that that the snow was very slow.

In the chemical world, when they are making moulds for high-end, precision tools, they have a special solvent that they use to stop the molecules of the item being moulded sticking to the inside of the mould. So, at a very sophisticated level, they are making sure that no parts of the two objects stick to each other and they use a solvent to do that.

So the executive suggested that the skiers use some of this solvent to stop the molecules of the snow sticking to the bottom of their skis. It was a perfectly legitimate and legal thing to do. As a result of this lucky intervention the team posted record times on the snow.

THE MESSAGE

That lubricant was subsequently developed into an industrial solvent that is now used for skis, and the name of that solvent actually has the executive's initials built into it as well, as the originator of the idea.

That is a perfect example of how to use your past to make a personal connection with your message. It was a little cameo of something that the executive had done, in his private, social, holiday life, to help illustrate innovation in action in the chemical world in a way that relates to people's lives. It was about reaching back into his personal background in order to be able to deliver something back to the business. Plus it had supporting visual evidence, a personally signed photograph of the gold medallist in the Olympics, which was a great prop to help validate the executive's message to the business.

Note that this particular story was not immediately obvious to the executive when we were initially discussing the message that they wanted to get across, or even when talking about storytelling or personally reaching out and connecting with content. It took some probing before we came up with the story.

So the idea is to try and panhandle through your past, in the same way the gold miners sifted through stream water hoping to turn up a gold nugget, you need to sift through your past, turning up stories and anecdotes.

Run through the narrative of your life, the rich tapestry of your existence (assuming it is not too threadbare), and find something from your world, whether it is sport, family, music, or previous work experience. find examples of teamwork or overcoming adversity or re-thinking and re-approaching a problem, all of these things that you could find in your hobbies, for example, that might actually fit into an organisational agenda or cause.

A different pair of glasses

There are many things that you can do to dredge up stories from your past. Obviously it helps if you keep a diary, or have a great memory. The trick is to be able to see past events in a different light.

You need to continually ask yourself, what parallels are there in what you see and do, what you have seen and done, to the messages that you are trying to get across.

The starting point is to thoroughly understand the value you are trying to crystallise for your message. What is it you are trying to get across? Is it a message about innovation, is it a message of overcoming adversity, is it a message about re-connecting with the customer?

Try and assess what the value being described by the message is, and then see if that value is or was present in other areas of your life, be it culture, sport or family. Are there any stories or anecdotes or cameos that you've come across in your life that will illustrate or paint a picture for people in that regard as well?

Unfortunately, some people will be reading this with a feeling of incomprehension because they do not have a life outside of work. If you are one of those people, if you do not have a life outside work, then we suggest that you get one – even if it is only for the good of your health.

It is absolutely true, that the people who are inspiring, who are able to personally connect, tend to be those have things outside of the work that they can draw on and bring to the table. It is very important that people have a work-life balance, not just for the life piece but also for the work piece as well.

THE MESSAGE

Seek personal and organisational mutuality

In order to deliver great effective messages in an authentic way within an organisational context, it is not enough to make a personal connection with the message. You also need to find some overlap, some alignment, between your personal life and your working life. You need your work and social life to mutually support and work with each other as well. So they both need to have their own centre of balance, but they do need to inform each other. In the modern world it is increasingly difficult, maybe impossible, to separate work and non-work. What individuals need to do is to align both work and non-work so that each supports the other. This means that their personal values, morals, motivating factors, align with work and working values and motivation.

The reason that this is important is that if there is no alignment between your personal values, and motivation, and work, you will appear inauthentic. You may well be able to connect with the message in a personal way, but you will not be able to in a way that also connects with your work, and so your message will not be persuasive.

One way of helping to find alignment is to start by asking, what is it that personally drives you in your work? Why did you join your organisation? What is it that inspires you about what it does, how it helps people, how it delivers to customers?

Try to find that moment of motivation, because quite often that can become buried and needs unearthing again. So you need to ask yourself, what is it that made this organisation great or good, why did you join, where is that moment, and try to visualise that moment. Why do you stay?

PERSONAL CONNECTIONS

And you need to try and find reasons, and force yourself to do this. People might snigger. They might think that the only reason they stay is because they have no choice. Well, frankly, that is not good enough, and if that is all you can find, then you will not come across as an authentic and inspiring communicator.

So you need to try and find and force yourself into positive reasons to do that, and those moments need to be visualised or crystallised. When we run the exercise on this subject and ask people what they enjoy about their organisation the typical response is about adding value to customer enterprise, or some similar response. But that is not what we are after. We are looking for a picture of an activity that sums up why it is such a good job to have.

Admittedly, there are inevitably downsides to work, stress, time pressure, bad bosses, difficult team members, the list goes on. It is the same for us. As a trainer, there is a lot of pressure, you are pushed for time, travel a lot, use up an awful lot of energy. But then there are those special moments that make you realise why you love doing the job.

Like the moment, one training session, when it was a lovely day, so we moved the class outside on the banks of the River Thames, and wandering down by the river, waiting for the participants to finish up, in the sunshine, it was suddenly obvious what a great job it was.

So you take those moments, those visual images and use those pictures to be an engine for your communications, to use that to re-inspire yourself each time, to remember what is great about the organisation that you work for and the job that you do.

What difference do you make?

As well as looking for the reasons why you joined the organisation, and why you stay with it, there is another factor you can draw inspiration from, to help your messages be more effective, and that is based on the difference you make.

So this part is about the impact that you have on people's lives, on the customer experience, and the way people view your organisation. It goes back to the maxim, popularised by Sumantra Ghoshal, the management guru, that the effective leader, or manager, is the one who looks beyond the things that would happen regardless of whether they turned up for work or not, to the difference that they make.

If you can assess where and how you make a difference to your organisation, you can use that to demonstrate your commitment to the organisation's cause, which one again will reinforce the authenticity of your message.

GET THE MESSAGE

- If your message does not persuade you, how will it persuade anyone else?

- You need to be immersed in your message. You need to be involved.

- Be aware that different cultures will react differently to your personal engagement with the message.

PERSONAL CONNECTIONS

- The more in-touch you are with your message, the more believable it is

- Panhandle through your past prospecting for personal connections with your message, and use those to connect with others.

- Try to cast a message related perspective on past events.

- Demonstrate how you have and will make and impact on the lives of others.

TWELVE

What's the Story?

Storytelling

The British entertainer Max Bygraves had a catchphrase: "I want to tell you a story". Not everyone was a fan of Bygraves, many considered his style lowbrow entertainment, but, like many other successful comedians, Bygraves knew something that many business executives have long forgotten – the power of storytelling.

Stories have fallen out of favour. Stories are stereotyped, they are fairy-tales told to children at bedtime, rambling dull anecdotes told over the table at a dinner party, ripping yarns told around the camp fire. Whether tear jerkers or happy endings, these narrative fictions have little or no association with the workplace, a world built on rational foundations.

Yet stories are one of the most effective communication tools and vehicles for messages that exist. But what makes a "good story", what elements should it possess, and why they are important? What about the storyteller, there is no story without the person telling the story after all, can a good story ever be truly independent of the person relating it? And what is the role of the story and the storyteller in business communications world, how can you make stories work for you in your organisation?

Just for kids?

Stories figure large in the world of children right across the world, whether they are bedtime stories, stories from cartoons, from comics, or those told by one child to another at school. There is a good reason for children's love of the story, asides from transporting them into a world of the imagination, because their stories are life stripped down to the essentials. There are complex moral and philosophical issues presented via simple messages woven into a tale.

As we get older while we are able to digest stories of greater complexity, at the same time we learn to associate stories with entertainment. Great works of literature, potboilers, Hollywood blockbusters, long running television soap operas, conventional operas, plays, musicals, all part of the entertainment industry.

Yet the more closely that stories are associated with entertainment, the more distanced they become from work and people fail to recognise how effective they are as communication tools in a variety of circumstances.

What makes a story?

French film director Jean-Luc Godard once famously said that a story should have a beginning, middle and an end, though not

WHAT'S THE STORY?

necessarily in that order. It is true that stories can come in many different forms, and if you asked people for examples of a great story, you are likely to get a range of responses.

Yet great stories do have some elements in common. A good story follows a sequence, not necessarily the obvious sequence, but a sequence nevertheless. Because order is important, allowing individuals to make sense of the story. A story should have a plot, and it should have characters, drawn from real life or from imagination.

This includes narratives told by people and businesses about themselves. These can be based on the past, about the present, or aspirational tales based on future goals and ambitions. Told in a variety of formats, they will usually be written down somewhere, although the individual content of the stories may change slightly from one communications medium to another.

The traditional story format, and the basic format adopted by Hollywood for films, is the three act story: set up; confrontation and resolution. Within this runs the narrative arc; the ups and downs of the story, mapping its high and low points.

Another way of breaking down the structure of the story into a number of discrete steps is one that we often use when talking about the story as a vehicle for messages, organisational or individual. There are six steps: the opening – this is the point where the key characters or entities are introduced; the build up- where the scene is set; the issues – which identifies the issues, objectives, obstacles which will form the subject of the story; events – how the plot unfolds through various events; the resolution – what happened in the end; and the ending – reflecting on what has happened, what it means, what can be learnt from the story.

Don't lose the plot

The plot is an essential element of a story. The plot must flow, and should not be too involved, unless the story is being delivered to a specialist audience. Transparency is important. The audience must want to know what happens next.

There are some classical plot models which are as valid today as they were hundreds of years ago, and worth noting. These include the struggle between good and evil, where good always prevails; the underdog story, where David beats Goliath; winning out in difficult circumstances; two people meet, there are obstacles, but love conquers all.

What relevance do these plotlines have to the business world? More than you might imagine.

Good versus bad could mean, profitability and value for shareholders, while fighting adverse market conditions, tough competitors, and hard to please customers. Or using the company's products to do some social good, like discovering a cure to an illness, or distributing products to communities in need. It can also mean developing a machine or gadget capable of liberating people from boring, repetitive, maybe painful and dangerous chores.

The underdog story is classic Virgin Group territory. Virgin and Richard Branson are well known for taking on lazy established companies that have dominated a market for long enough to forget what offering value and good service means. It is the Apple versus Microsoft story; the Virgin Group against BA; Ben and Jerry's against Unilever (which was eventually acquired by its larger rival).

WHAT'S THE STORY?

Then there is the against all odds stories, where the checkout boy becomes the CEO, or the small company rises to lead its market, or it fights off an unwelcome suitor, or narrowly avoids bankruptcy and then becomes successful. Alternatively, the company may produce a product that was thought technically impossible.

As for love conquering all, there are more than enough tales of corporate mergers, although a happy outcome is not always guaranteed.

The plot must be woven around characters, and the longer the story the more characters that can be used. However, it is important to make the characters recognisable. People need to be able to engage with the characters, to empathise with the characters and, consequently, the plot. Both should be relevant.

Long enough, short enough

Whereas a good story can be of any length, short or of epic proportions, in the world of modern messages, a world of limited time and attention spans, shorter stories, or at least in short, bite-sized instalments are better.

Brevity is also good for leaving the audience wanting more. Because, although the long, drawn-out narrative, with many characters and sub-plots is of little use for modern messages, there are many great epic stories which are just a collection of shorter stories, woven together.

THE MESSAGE

Message memo: The plot thickens – the Story Grid

Flesh out the plot by using the following grid to help work through the various elements of the story.

Story Element	Plot Components (What points, facts or events do we have to support this plot element);	Characters Who can we identify as characters in this role: This might be • Specific individuals, [leaders]; • Business area; • A brand; • External party [eg market; NGO, private equity].
A: Present State Credible and compelling account of where we are now – and what is wrong with alternative visions. Could contain: i} Opening: introduce characters or entities ii) Build up: set the scene		
B: Plot Development Portrayal of the journey; obstacles to be overcome; the dramatic tension. Could contain: i) Issue: what went wrong ii) Event:: what happened next		
C: End Point Vision of where we can get to: opportunities, values, pay-offs that successful change can deliver. Could contain: i) Resolution ii) Lessons		

WHAT'S THE STORY?

Storytellers

A bad story teller can ruin even the best of stories. How you tell the story is up to you. You need to find a style that you are comfortable with. Fortunately there a number of different approaches to choose from.

Personality and demeanour is important, and will affect the way that your material is received. One style is to take the main elements of your story and relate them, as far as possible, without comment or elaboration. Another approach is to prepare a rough framework or skeleton structure, then use that framework as the foundations of the story, and embellish it by improvising, taking diversions, adding and subtracting material as you see fit.

You can attempt a more theatrical approach, being dramatic with your delivery, use examples that stretch belief –while remaining true to your core message, and bearing in mind issues, already discussed in this book, such as credibility and authenticity. At the opposite end of the story telling scale, you could deliver your material in a comparatively unemotional, dead-pan, factual manner.

Important elements in the delivery of the story include register -the vocal tones used, non verbal gestures, phrasing and pace of delivery, and the type of language used. It is also important to find the idiom when talking to an audience with people from different cultural or linguistic backgrounds.

Roll up roll up!

One great storyteller was Phineas T. Barnum, the huckster promoter of *The Greatest Show On Earth* and father of the public relations industry. Barnum was a brilliant communicator, salesman and showman. He invented the beauty contest, the baby contest, and the travelling show. He popularised the theatre, introducing the matinee performance. Most famous for running Barnum's American Museum and the Barnum and Bailey Circus, he always ensured the consumer experience lived up to his hyperbole.

Barnum's success was founded on an innate understanding of the power of the story, revealed through a number of his activities. As a journalist his populist streak and lack of legal knowledge landed him with a 60 days jail sentence, yet the story of his release was one of triumph marked, as it was, by a marching band, and a troop of 40 horses.

Barnum told stories through spectacle, whether it was the American Museum in New York, PT Barnum's Grand Travelling Museum, Menagerie, Caravan, and Hippodrome, or The Greatest Show On Earth, as it became known, or "The Towering Monarch of His Mighty Race, Whose Like the World Will Never See Again," – Jumbo, the elephant.

He also created a story for his living exhibits to provide them with more substance, and make them appear more interesting. So Joice Heth was 161 years old and the former nurse of George Washington, American president #1, and as Barnum described Heth in his posters: "Unquestionably the most astonishing and interesting curiosity in the world!"

With his autobiography, *How I made Millions*, Barnum also tapped into the power of the inspirational story, with a tacit promise that it was possible to unlock the secrets of Barnum's success and achieve success by reading his book.

WHAT'S THE STORY?

Credibility

Barnum's success also emphasised the importance of credibility when storytelling, or indeed delivering any type of message. One reason Barnum succeeded is that people believed him when he told them some implausible tale, that one of the exhibits in his museum was an embalmed "Feejee Mermaid," for example, and not half monkey, half dried fish as it was in reality.

True the public wanted to believe the things that Barnum told them, but they also bought into the showman appearance, and the self perpetuated hype that surrounded his career as a showman, impresario, and museum owner.

In the same way, telling a story in business context still requires you to have the appropriate credentials. Art Fry is a retired chemical engineer who used to work at the conglomerate 3M, he sang in a choir in his part time, and was looking for a way to mark pages in his hymn book –paper bookmarks just fell out. So Fry decided to use a weak adhesive invented by another 3M researcher Spencer Silver (who was actually searching for a strong adhesive) to temporarily attach a bookmark to different pages. Then he used it to stick paper on a report when he was marking it. Post-it notes had been invented.

It is a great story, especially if told by Fry, the chemical engineer, as opposed to 3M's corporate spokesperson. So if you want to tell a story, make sure you have the right credentials for the story you choose.

Message memo: What's the story?

It doesn't take much imagination, to see how classic storylines fit with different organisations or individuals. When it comes to plots there are a certain number of basic plotlines and then variations of them. Exactly how many basic plots there are is debatable but here are a few of the principal ones:

The Quest – where the main character(s) have to meet an objective, often within a limited time period. The target of the quest varies, it might be to destroy the ring, as in the Tokien's Lord of the Rings, or to become number one in your market, reach a particular sales target, increases sales margins to a certain figure, expand into new territories, obtain a promotion, or get a new job.

Overcoming adversity – The main character(s) face insurmountable odds, yet, faced with such a challenge, eventually triumph over adversity. Adversity often comes in the form of a particular adversary, in the classic David versus Goliath clash. This type of story may involve a small company outperforming a much larger rival, and innovative business capturing a market, an executive who has made it to the top table, seeing off rivals. This may also involve the sub-plot of the Comeback Kid, the organisation that is performing badly until it manages a successful turnaround, like Lou Gerstner's rescue of IBM.

Rags to riches – Similar in some ways to the overcoming adversity story, the main character comes from nothing, or next to nothing, to make good. Often the journey involves stumbling after some early, quick wins, and then having to firmly establish a position at the top. Amazon.com is a good example of a small start up that has become a huge successful organisation with a few hiccups along the way. Henry Ford started off constructing a prototype automobile in an outbuilding.

WHAT'S THE STORY?

Storytelling, business, and the message

This book is about communication and the message, and that is the context within which stories are useful for organisations and individuals in the business context.

Stories are a package that contains the message, the value proposition. Storytelling is a way of delivering messages to a target audience. Messaging can and should aim to mould the audience so that it buys into the proposition. Storytelling is about preparing the ground.

As we have seen messaging is an assertion plus some evidence to support that assertion. Storytelling is a package within which we can deliver the message, and it is instructive to see how, over the years, technology has had a big impact on the packaging of that message.

The use of stories as packages for business propositions has long been a part of advertising, for example. In the 1920s Procter and Gamble of Cincinnati used the radio, a new technology at the time, to promote their cleaning products. There were numerous small commercial radio stations, but all had difficulty in filling their schedules, especially during the day. Then Procter and Gamble hit upon the idea of sponsoring fifteen-minute entertainment and drama slots, rather than just running conventional advertising.

The content that ran in these radio slots tended to be melodramatic, and with the products placed centre-stage in the story. At the end of each episode an announcer told the audience that the programme had been sponsored by Procter and Gamble. Thus was born the soap opera, the term reflecting the juxtaposition of culture and domestic drudgery.

In time other companies copied Procter and Gamble and sponsored their own soap operas and these became a feature of twentieth century American consumer culture. Each episode formed part of an apparently interminable series.

In the 1950s soap operas made a seamless transition from radio to television, with the only major format change being an extension from 15 to 30 minutes in length. Procter and Gamble continued to support the format, sponsoring one of the most successful soap operas of the 1960s, *The Doctors*, which ran for nearly twenty years, becoming truly international, by the time of the last episode in 1983. Today, some soaps are still sponsored, but the ties between predict and story are weaker. Nevertheless, soap operas demonstrate the capacity of technology to deliver a story, and the messages it contains, to a global audience.

Business stories

Soap operas are stories that use plots written about other people's lives. But stories can be just as powerful and effective communication devices when they are told by the business about itself; whether it is via speeches from the CEO, or copy on the website.

In all corporate storytelling, you need to pay attention to the audience. It has to be the right audience for the story, with a correlation between audience and story; what suits one audience will not suit another. So target stories appropriately.

Also monitor audience reaction. In person, it is easy to see if you have talked for too long, or lost your audience. There are tell-tale signs whether it is mass yawning, or a noticeable rise in audience noise.

Much of the storytelling today, however, happens in the virtual world of the internet. Instead of sitting in front of you, the virtual audience is out there somewhere in the world at the end of a broadband connection.

And while you may not be able to see if the individuals in your audience are shifting in their seats from boredom, there are ways to find out how your audience is responding to your messages.

Web designers, and IT departments, have an array of tools available to monitor web traffic over a range of criteria, from page views to how long individuals spend in particular areas of a websites and the routes that they take through websites.

In addition you can use marketing research to assess impact of a website and its contents. There are also feedback mechanisms which allow visitors to post up comments. Perhaps unsurprisingly in more connected world the communication flow is much more two way than it ever used to be, so do not be surprised to get considerable audience input via comment.

Cultural sensitivities

We have touched upon cultural awareness in other chapters, and indeed many cultures have a long and rich story telling tradition.

Audiences differ around the world, even within the same country. This is where cultural differences come into play. You must be certain that the story and the messages within it resonate for your audience. When you are storytelling in person, it is often a good idea to demonstrate that you are culturally aware by incorporating appropriate cultural reference, either into the story itself or the introduction. Remember, however, that you must retain authenticity, and not attempt to "adopt" another culture as part of your persona.

With a website it is important to be aware of the signals that are sent out aside from the text. The impact of a captivating and persuasive story, with well constructed messages can be reduced by culturally insensitive graphics or navigation.

Stories from messages

Good stories can be made up of many messages, or just one. Take the Dow Chemical example. As we have seen, the company faced a backlash in the 1970s over its production of napalm used with horrifying effect in the Vietnam War. As a result the company's chairman Carl Gerstacker sought to push the message of involvement in "life sciences" – with the emphasis on life.

This message formed part of a story in which Dow Chemical was committed to life and creation. It had pioneered drugs which saved lives. The story here was of a company not only carrying out positive research and production, but overseeing the administering of these products to communities who reaped the benefits. This story was based on one message.

The message came first. The story can then be retold through company publications and other promotion material, as well as

WHAT'S THE STORY?

Message memo: Chinese challenge

With over a billion eager consumers waiting to snap up their products, it is no surprise that the issue of how to use messages effectively in China is high on the agenda of Western based multinational corporations, and their advertising agencies.

Research by Nader Tavassoli, professor of marketing, at London Business School highlights the challenge that Western companies face trying to enter markets in China.

It transpires that a different approach is required to get over the brand message in China from that in the US or the UK. With over 10,000 logographs each corresponding to a single spoken syllable, the Chinese language is visually rich in a way that English is not.

For maximum impact when creating branding and advertising messages in Chinese, marketers should be aware of a number of issues, says Tavassoli. Reading logographs involves more visual processing. Consequently, visual features, such as colours assume greater significance in branding.

Equally, Chinese consumers are more sensitive to the fonts used. So for example, Chinese consumers are more attuned to the perceived femininity or masculinity of fonts. Use a masculine font to advertise a new lipstick and sales may not meet expectations.

The spatial location of design elements assumes greater significance to a Chinese consumer. And so changes in design layout may trigger unexpected responses.

Finally, marketing best practice in the West holds that referencing

> the brand name verbally early on in any advertisings or marketing material is important in terms of creating lasting impression. In China, however, says Tavassoli, the order in which verbal information is presented is not so important.
>
> Style it seems, is as important as substance, when it comes to composing ads in China.

advertising. Similarly, there is no reason why businesses cannot take a story or group of stories about their actions in the present, combined with corporate vision about the future, as a source for messages. These can then be embedded in popular consumer culture.

Getting the story out

Storytellers can now call on a plethora of media to get their stories out into the world.

In addition to traditional communication channels, such as the print and broadcast media, we can now add more recent technological innovations such as podcasting, instant messaging, mobile phones, video casting, and many others.

The internet gives an opportunity to project corporate image and stories in a more distinct way. Web pages offer scope for passing on business stories, utilising rich media, such as slide shows and video. The interconnectedness of stories with a central story-line can be enhanced through embedded links.

WHAT'S THE STORY?

Web pages may be graphically pleasing to the eye, but they should also be functional and informative. They are there to provide messages. Good websites must also give good, accurate and trustworthy information. Case studies are one effective way of authenticating messages.

Case Studies

No business should pass up the chance to tell well-crafted stories about itself, and one good way doing this is through the publication of case studies.

A particular genre within business storytelling, case studies are a good means of telling your audience about that most prized of corporate possessions: the satisfied customer. Plus, as case studies are factual they carry more weight with sceptical audiences. They are also an excellent way of countering any negative publicity.

When preparing a case study the authors have to be aware that although they are telling a story, there is no room for taking liberties with the truth. The information used must be entirely factual, and should be rigorously researched for its accuracy. And, if you are going to reference clients or customers, make sure that you obtain their consent in advance.

At an individual level the case study becomes the equivalent of the resume. A quick trawl of the web reveals that many people now use personal websites, and blogs, to create a story about their working and personal life, which they can use to deliver messages, whether they are furthering their career, drubbing up work, or merely gaining support for a cause that they believe in.

Our storytellers

Businesses need good storytellers, people who are able to craft convincing and compelling content, whether it is used to promote the company, its activities, or its products and services.

Although contemporary storytellers are often going to be the people working in corporate communications, it is vital that everyone in the organisation is aware of what stories are being told.

So if the company is recounting a story in which it takes a very serious attitude to environmental stewardship, everyone within the firm should try to support that story, not only at work, but where possible through the way that they behave in their everyday lives. So, if a facility causes a lot of pollution, or takes a careless attitude towards litter or waste, this will reduce the credibility of the overall story.

Not this one again!

Storytelling is not about sentiment. It is about pursuing corporate goals, and a certain degree of creativity will be required to ensure that the audience receives the corporate story in the right frame of mind.

Many people, certainly in the West, appear to be tremendously cynical about aspects of corporate life, whether it is businesses' commitment to corporate social responsibility (CSR), or the claims companies make of their products.

So if you are promote your business using stories and messages you will need to combat this cynicism if you are to succeed. Sometimes, it seems as if all the angles on a story have already been covered, and it is almost impossible to achieve any differentiation. It is true that many of the stories that companies are telling today seem to be remarkably similar.

Most companies are, for example, committed to upholding the highest standards of environmental management. Some may even be able to offer evidence of years of commitment to these policies, including awards from third parties such as international non-governmental organisations.

Yet often such CSR activities will be dismissed as greenwash, an attempt to wash over the environmental damage that a company is doing, despite its assertions sophisticated or otherwise to the contrary.

There are a number of ways of dealing with such criticism, persistence is one, evidence another, but what certainly helps is to try and repackage the story is that it does not appear like the countless others being told by corporations around the world, some of which appear not to be so socially and environmentally conscious after all. Differentiation might be as simple as not using the obvious "environmental commitment" title, or associating the story visually with acres of the colour green. A little creativity is required.

We are not alone

Unfortunately corporate storytellers are no longer the only raconteurs in the tribal hut. Today the stories and messages emanating from companies have to compete with the hundreds of other stories and messages that their intended audience will encounter during the average day.

The veracity and the truthfulness of the stories you are telling will be under constant attack from a number of different quarters, such as competitors and pressure groups. The undermining of your own stories will occasionally be overt, but is much more likely to be by other asserting different versions of a similar story. Plus the effectiveness of your story and its messages will be diluted buy countless other similar messages.

While it is important to be aware of the external environment, who is doing what, and what works particularly well and what doesn't, it is a mistake to constantly change the story to suit events. Just because a certain line taken by one company appears to be doing particularly well, that is no reason to copy it, especially if that line is out of kilter with the stories that your were expressing previously. Too much flexibility leads to charges of inconsistency.

And the same goes for personal storytelling. Be sure to review the stories that you are telling periodically, to hone, revise, and fine tune them, maybe to throw out some older less successful stories and replace them with some new material. Do not, however, make the mistake of following the fashionable story merely for the sake of it. It is a sure way to lose authenticity and credibility, and very quickly too.

No short-cuts

There should be nothing haphazard about the use of stories. If they are part of a firm's history and background, they must be shaped to

WHAT'S THE STORY?

make them relevant. Considerable care must always be taken in their development and use.

Business still faces a major challenge in using stories, but it is a challenge that must be faced. A story that creates impact is much more successful than any amount of messages. Great stories succeed by being memorable, they are adopted by the audience as their own, and in this way they cement the value proposition.

GET THE MESSAGE

- Storytelling is not just for kids; it is a very useful device for getting across your messages.

- Use the story grid to help map out your story.

- Be aware of the basic story structure of and the different plots.

- Remember the success of a story is just as much in the telling as it is in the content of the story.

- You will need a well thought through and powerful story to compete with all the other stories vying for attention.

THE MESSAGE

Twenty Key Ideas

If you have read the book, even part of it, you will appreciate by now both the important role of the message, how creating effective messages can improve individual and organisational communication and performance, and the challenges involved in creating good messages.

Here to help, though, are 20 key ideas from the book which should prove a useful aide-mémoire:

1. In a world where advances in technology mean that people are bombarded with information and messages from a multiplicity of sources, attention spans are growing shorter by the day; unless messages are very well crafted, they will be ignored.

2. Think about reaching the millennial generation, and dealing with the "so what" question.

3. Information on its own is not a message. A fact on its own is not a message.

THE MESSAGE

4. A message is a collection of words, actions, designs, images, sounds which creates an assertion that is supported by compelling evidence. Or in short hand: a message = assertion (or less frequently a command or question) + evidence.

5. Messages contain three important elements: the active ingredient; the behavioural change; and the example.

6. You need to be authentic. If you are not believable, no one will believe your message.

7. Consistency counts. Saying a few things often is likely to have more impact than a lot of uncoordinated messages – which is just confusing.

8. Three important types of message are: the context message; the news hook message; and the call to action message.

9. And two important types of example: the hearts and minds example, appealing to the emotional part of our mind; and the data example, appealing to the rational.

10. In a message campaign you should aim to attract and recruit both grassroots activists and opinion leaders.

11. The Message Grid is a harmonising tool that allows you to coordinate and harmonise messages across three strands of leadership: product leadership; market leadership; and thought leadership.

TWENTY KEY IDEAS

12. Remember to target intermediaries and watch out for maverick communicators.

13. Use frames to move the discussion onto the territory that you want.

14. Messages are not passive, or one way. They are about participation, conversations and transactions. It takes two – or more.

15. To inspire others with your messages, you need passion, charisma and credibility.

16. Make a personal connection with your message. People buy people.

17. Seek organisational and personal alignment to make messages that are more powerful and that work for you on a personal level too.

18. Show your audience how you make a difference, to back up your messages.

19. Stories are a very effective package for messages.

20. Brevity is best.

Gerry Griffin

Gerry was formerly head of training at Burson Marsteller, and Director of Communications at the London Business School. He has almost 20 years experience with a broad range of communication specialism. Author of five previous business books: *The Power Game* (looking at corporate power struggles) *Dot Con* (dealing with Internet strategy); *Reputation Management* (looking at the world of corporate reputations and their impact on the bottom line); *Games Companies Play* – which looks at office dynamics – and *Fools Gold* – cautionary tales of speculation. Gerry has trained a wide number of FTSE 100 and Fortune 500 companies.

Gerry is founder and CEO of Business Communication Forum and also mobile of learning agency: Skill-Pill M Learning

Check out: www.thebcf.com and www.skill-pill.com

Andrew Lark

Andrew's 22 years experience across business-to-business and consumer sectors spans building successful businesses and leading award-winning marketing programs and teams for Fortune and Times 100 companies, global technology brands, start-ups and the world's hottest advertising and communications agencies.

During his career he has worked and lived in the majority of the world's major markets and developed a reputation as a highly creative executive, marketing turn-around specialist, entrepreneur and authority on social media. He is a prolific writer, blogger and speaker on marketing, emerging business strategies, marketing/communications measurement, and Web 2.0.

Today, Andrew is vice president, Dell, where he is charged with leading global marketing for its Large Enterprise group – both the largest within Dell and the industry. Prior to this he lead communications, conversations and global online – with responsibility for Dell.com – the world's largest eCommerce site. During this time he spearheaded the company's revitalization of it's online presence – including it's highly acclaimed social media strategies.